LESSONS FROM THE
12
ARCHANGELS

LESSONS FROM THE
12
ARCHANGELS

Divine Intervention in Daily Life

BELINDA J. WOMACK

Bear & Company
Rochester, Vermont • Toronto, Canada

Bear & Company
One Park Street
Rochester, Vermont 05767
www.BearandCompanyBooks.com

Bear & Company is a division of Inner Traditions International

Library of Congress Cataloging-in-Publication Data
Womack, Belinda, 1961–
  Lessons from the twelve archangels : divine intervention in daily life / Belinda J.
Womack.
    pages cm
  Includes index.
  Summary: "A powerful guide to open your life to the wisdom and healing of the
Angels and their love for us"—Provided by publisher.
  ISBN 978-1-59143-323-1 (pbk.)
  1. Angels. 2. Archangels. 3. Spiritual life. I. Title.
  BL477.W66 2015
  202'.15—dc23

2015011954

Printed and bound by CPI Group (UK) Ltd, Croydon CR0 4YY

10 9 8 7 6 5 4 3 2 1

Text design by Priscilla Baker and layout by Virginia Scott Bowman
This book was typeset in Garamond Premier Pro with Poetica, Gill Sans, Snell
Roundhand, and Helvetica used as display typefaces

To send correspondence to the author of this book, mail a first-class letter to the
author c/o Inner Traditions • Bear & Company, One Park Street, Rochester, VT
05767, and we will forward the communication, or contact the author directly at
www.BelindaWomack.com.

For Robert Davidson: thank you for your friendship and faith in these great Angels.

Contents

ANGEL TREASURY

ANGEL MESSAGES

ANGEL LETTERS

Foreword

When asked to write a foreword, one can usually rely on the author's thought processes to comment on the work. And can logically extrapolate from the text and explain, using left brain signposts, what the author is trying to say. Then, one can encourage the reader to take a leisurely walk through the work, knowing that the reader will come out at the end with something to hang his or her reasoning hat on.

But with Belinda Womack's marvelous book this is not possible. While I can easily say that the whole arc of the work is about getting rid of fear and surrendering to intuition, this will not help you to grasp what the author is all about. To do so, you and I must throw out our anchors, our preconceived ideas. Instead, we are asked to believe that Angels are real, that they are active forces in our lives—asked to believe that we can learn to communicate with them in clear, precise ways that will help us to live better lives. We are exhorted to listen to the Sound and Light of the Divine, the music of another realm, heard sometimes in dreams or daydreaming, reminding us that Heaven is here *now*, that we don't need to wait until we die to find its consolations.

Heaven and Earth are one, we are told. But we are like little children lost in a crowd, believing that our parents have abandoned us and left us to fend on our own. Fear comes from our belief in our separation from God. And why must we experience this fear? Because we must learn to grow into the knowledge of our own resilience and power, our ability to be creators like God and to manifest the life we want. The experience of separation was programmed into the Earth experiment. We are taught that this world of duality is a school of development, an obstacle course created for our greater benefit and joy. We are here to know—in the biblical sense of knowing—that God's truth is love, that in applying love to all our encounters in this world, we resolve the separation. Realizing that all is love, we become godlike. All of us are ascended masters in the making. We are polishing God's mirror until Oneness is reconquered.

The voice that speaks to us with such compassionate understanding of our dilemmas is the voice of the Twelve Archangels of the Central Soul, the powers that govern this world. They wish us well, they love us, and they want us to succeed. Their communications come through teachings (the "Angel Treasury"), messages (forty-eight of them), and letters. They speak through a vehicle so clear and pure that you cannot doubt her authenticity and her authority. Belinda has learned to get out of the way so that we can hear the twelve great teachers. Yet her sweet and powerful voice reminds us at every page of the work she has done on herself to always make room for the Divine, and thus to be of service to us, her readers.

Who is Belinda? She says she is a messenger. The "twelve big guns," as she often calls them, appear to her in many guises, including hula-skirts and ridiculous hair fashions. They are Christian sometimes, sometimes rabbis or Buddhas, male or female. That doesn't matter. What matters is that they talk through her and she makes herself hollow, like a singing reed, to their voices and their teachings.

I have known Belinda for nineteen years, and never have I heard her speak other than the truth, even if I didn't want to hear it. Always what has come through her has been unadulterated! She is very humble but she magnetizes a power so intense and clear that anyone reading her or listening to her experiences something of the Sound and Light of the Divine that she is speaking of. The authority that rings through her words is what makes me pick up my pen and write to you, the reader, to let go and let her words sing within you.

You will not only hear messages of "loving-kindness," which is what the great Archangels say they are sending us, but you will be given the tools to practice and to achieve transformation. These are mainly easy visualizations, color tools, and simple affirmations that anyone can practice. Try them. They work! You will also be given a glossary of terms that clarify many complex ideas in simple and concise language. I love the glossary! Her approach to God (Mother Father God), the chakras, your karma, the human Soul, male and female, the inner child, are unique visions that differ from anything you will read in other books in the spiritual literature. What you get is original channeled material. Her words flow like a crystalline river whose source she entices you to find. Follow her words, open the book anywhere you are guided to, plunge into the world she lives in, and you will begin to get the taste of Oneness.

CATHERINE SHAINBERG

Catherine Shainberg, Ph.D., is a psychologist, healer, and teacher with a private practice in New York City. In 1982 she founded the School of Images (www .schoolofimages.com), dedicated to teaching the revelatory dream and *kavanah* (intent) techniques of the ancient Sephardic Kabbalah tradition. She conducts imagery and dreaming workshops internationally.

Note on the Glossary

At the end of this book you will find a glossary of important words and terms that arise in the text. The glossary is a tool to support your understanding of the Angels' language as they intend it. The first time a glossary term appears in this book, it will be in bold. You may find that your understanding of certain words or terms is different from the way the Angels use them. As you work your way through this book, feel free to access the glossary at any time. Perusing the glossary is not only fun but a quick way to shift from a negative state of mind to a blissful one.

Preface

Communicating
with Angels

I have always believed in the presence of **Angels**.

I have a memory from my birth of being wheeled quickly down a long hospital corridor. I can remember the painful sounds and hurtful lights, the smell of antiseptic, the whiteness of the nurse's clothing. I can remember, as if it was yesterday, a strange sense of shock and wonder of being back on **Earth**. And then I saw them, the magnificent Beings of **Sound** and **Light** surrounding me. I remember their happy colors and soft singing. I can clearly recall their smiling faces and the great comfort they provided. They stayed with me during the long hours I would spend in nature as a young child. It was in the forest that my **imagination** worked the best and I could **see** beyond the limits of this mundane plane. During my early years, I was certainly an intuitive "right brainer" (using the creative and emotional centers of one's brain).

When I turned eleven I decided that I wanted to be a scientist. When I turned twelve I remember hearing a huge door slam shut in my head. The Angels lived on the other side of that door because I was no longer able to see them, or communicate with them. However, I never stopped asking for their help. I grew up, studied to become a biologist and believed I would be working in a research lab for the rest of my life. Although I was sensitive to the needs and feelings of others, I was a dedicated "left brainer" (using the logical and rational centers of one's brain). I worked in a university medical facility where another human's life might depend on my precision and accuracy.

One day while separating lymphocytes from a child's bone marrow sample, I had the out-of-body experience of leaving the sterile hood I was working in and entering a stone room. The room was round and had no ceiling. Through the ceiling a great beam of light revealed that an Angel was watching me. **Archangel** Gabriel blew a trumpet in my ear and spoke to me, loud and clear, inside my mind. Gabriel's message made my entire body shake. The Angel said that I was being called to do a new kind of work. I was going to help **human beings** connect with their divinity. After I received Gabriel's message, I was shocked to find myself still holding the syringe in one hand and plastic sample vial in the other. Surely, hours had passed, if not years while I had traveled into my right brain and had an Archangel reawaken the creative centers of my mind. My initial response was that I was having a nervous break-down. I must be crazy. And yet, I could still operate a flow cytometer, run my experiments, and communicate like a "normal" person.

Angels communicate through a clear knowing that comes into my mind and I "just know." This knowing is united with the feeling of unconditional and total love. They do not speak in a voice other than the same voice I hear when talking to myself. It is a distinct communi-cation that comes with absolute clarity and indescribable love. Angelic communication requires a fusion between my rational thinking centers, or left brain, and my creative and emotional centers, or right brain. My hypothesis, which I cannot prove, is that I can converse with Angels because my childhood demanded I develop both the left and right brain faculties in order to survive my environment. My **Soul** tells me that my communicating with the Twelve Archangel Kingdoms was always a part of the divine plan, and my destiny in this life.

Perhaps the best way to describe the accuracy required in Angelic communication is to have a musician describe how he or she tunes an instrument. A talented musician must know when a note is being played out of key. My best friend, Robert, is such a musician. When he hears a sound that is out of tune, you would think someone ran over his foot with a truck. It is the same way when I communicate with an Angel. If I am not hearing the message correctly and recording it precisely, I feel contraction in my body. I cannot breathe because I am hearing "notes being played out of key."

Writing with Angels is a partnership. We write together. They send me their teachings through my **intuition** (knowing). I then translate the message into language. This task requires the use of both my right brain and left brain. It is a back-and-forth process of receiving the teaching using the sensory centers in my creative brain while testing the precision and accuracy of the language with my scientific and rational brain. Angelic communication comes through at the vibration of **Heaven**, a place where **fear** cannot exist. This is why I choose to capitalize the "a" in "Angels." I do this to demonstrate that their vibration is higher than our own. There is a high magic that happens when human eyes see this word—it raises the vibration of **ego** to that of Soul. I capitalize "Soul" for the same purpose.

When I write together with Angels, I must shift the vibration of my thoughts and feelings to match that of unconditional love. The Angels rely on me to present them with the most common problems we humans face. I communicate the problems to them. They give me the answers. This is how we write together: I am the Earth. They are the Heaven. I must rise up to Heaven. They must come to Earth through my right brain. Creating this kind of composition feels like falling in love. It is pure euphoric bliss. I am greatly blessed.

My belief is that everyone has the ability to communicate with Angels. This requires moving ego out of the way and jumping fully into the magical world of the right brain. It helps to "come as a child" because the **Divine Child** within us rules the **superconscious**, or highest vibration thought center inside us. My star pupils are always children. Ask a child to walk through the purple door, leave behind his logic, and enter into his creative imagination. Watch the joy on his face as he experiences instant success with seeing, hearing, and trusting his Angels. I invite you to move your ego into the back room, open your creative mind and experience the infinite love, color, and truthful communication of Angels. I am forever grateful to coauthor with them!

LOVE ETERNAL,

BELINDA

Acknowledgments

My heart is rich with gratitude for both the Divine and human assistance that have gone into the creation of this book. Thank you, Jane Lahr, for your editing wizardry and clear vision. I am forever grateful to my publicist and friend, Eileen Duhne, for her talent, patience, and love.

Truly, I feel blessed to have the patient expertise of the gifted staff of Inner Traditions • Bear & Co. Thank you all for bringing *Lessons from the Twelve Archangels* to life!

Thank you Soul family, Catherine Shainberg, Fanny and Robert Davidson, Val Cowett, and my husband, Michael Wolk, for your love and support.

And, my family, without you I could not be my authentic self. Thank you Marvyn and Jack for bringing me into this incarnation. Thank you brilliant brothers, sister, cousins, aunts, uncles, nieces, nephew, and ancestry. I am grateful!

Thank you clients and students for your commitment to transforming layer after layer of what separates us from God. I am grateful to each of you and I trust that you feel my love and gratitude. May the healing love of the Twelve Archangels continue to support us every step of the journey!

ANGEL TREASURY

Inspiration
and Practical Application

The "Angel Treasury," six chapters or "books," is a treasure box of self-help tools that delivers a miraculous and **healing** quality when used for daily meditation. My inspiration for the Treasury comes from many years of working with individual clients. It is my mission, with the Twelve Archangels, to get to the deepest roots of my client's suffering as quickly as possible. I remember one client that I was blessed to help nearly twenty years ago. She told me that the insight I gave her and the tools I provided to transform the old hurt were truly miraculous. This client shared that in one hour I had covered more ground and made more progress than she had experienced working twenty-five years with her therapist. Please understand: I am not a psychologist. My role in supporting clients is to help them tap into their own healing ability. I do this by working as a spiritual messenger. I communicate with the **wounded child (subconscious)** within them in the same way that I communicate with Angels. I offer clients what I hear and encourage them in making their own decisions as to what to do with the information. The guided imagery exercises in the Angel Treasury are the same that I use to guide the **transformation** when my clients are open and ready for healing. Their healing comes from the **higher self.** I am the messenger, con-

necting the guidance of Heaven to their life experiences on Earth.

This is the power held within the Angel Treasury! It contains wisdom that helps the mind to surrender to a greater love and sustenance. It carries the love of the Angels in every word so that when read, this love is absorbed into the mind of the reader and supports the letting go of layers of the deepest wounds.

Each of the six books builds on the one before it, lifting us higher in vibration and carrying us deeper into our connection with God. We need to remember this connection and allow our lives to be filled with our divinity. I believe we would treat each other with much greater respect if we could embrace that we are the divine children of our Creator. We are all learning how to move from being human *to* becoming human beings.

I invite you to explore this treasure trove of Angelic guidance and discover the great wealth of healing powers held inside of you.

Book 1

Where Does God's Energy Come From?

Asking where **God** comes from is asking your own mind, heart, body, and Soul, "Where do I come from and what am I made out of?" Angels and humans and stars and oceans and black space in the night sky are all made of the same substance Angels call **energy**.

God is energy, and this energy is the substance of all that is physical and nonphysical as well. God's energy or divine essence or spirit is exactly what God is made of and where God comes from. We will tell you much about this mystical circle, a circle without a beginning or end, a circle that breathes in and out in a most magnificent spiral of color.

Energy creates Light and Sound, and Light and Sound are what God is made of, and Light and Sound are where God comes from, and you do, too. The Sound and Light are always together; Sound creates **emotion**, and Light creates **thought**.

In God are both Mother (Divine Emotion) and Father (Divine Thought), Sound, and Light. **Mother God** and **Father God** together created **Divine Love**, and Divine Love desired to expand God out from the realms of spirit, thought, and emotion to the physical, and so **Creation** began. God is made of emotion, thought, love, and Creation; this is where God comes from, and you do, too.

Energy, Sound and Light, emotion, thought, love, and Creation create the heart of God. God's heart is filled with Divine Love, which means God has no conditions, no rules or standards for loving. Each and every particle of God's energy is filled with Divine Love, and love connects each particle of energy to every other particle of energy, which we call the experience of **Oneness**.

Oneness is a vibration of perfect unity, a complete connection of thought with **feeling** of love and Creation. Oneness allows each particle of God's energy to hear and feel the thoughts and feelings of every other particle of energy. This would feel like you have complete compassion and insight into every human being you meet, or rock, tree, animal, or drop of water you touch.

ORIGINS

Mother and Father and Divine Love and Creation make up the whole essence of God's energy. God sent forth the energy, the Sound and Light in the name of Oneness, and manifested the **Universe**. The Universe is made of many particles all capable of sensing each other because Oneness connects them to the Center of God.

The **center** of God's energy is called the **Central Soul or Sun**, and from the Central Soul, all Creation originates. God's energy moves out as a spiral of color from the center, and the spiral has an infinite number of rings of energy, Sound, and Light. From the Central Sun, twelve Suns were created, and from these Suns or Souls of God's energy came all the galaxies, stars, planets, and Beings of Love. It is difficult for us to try to describe God's Creation because we see no **separation**. Even saying twelve Suns come from the Central Sun implies each of these Suns is separate. It is more like taking white Light and shining it through a prism to show twelve colors or rays of Light and twelve Sounds all originating from one Sound. When you take each of these twelve Lights and Sounds and generate twelve more from each one, you then have 144

Lights and Sounds. When mixed and played together like an orchestra filled with 144 different instruments, you can imagine how infinite God's creativity is.

Each and every particle of energy originates from the Central Soul and has memory of the center. Each particle is a sentient Being of Light and Sound. Every moon, planet, asteroid, and star is a thinking, feeling, loving, and creating Being of God. Each has its own center, its own Soul, which connects back to the Central Soul of God.

THE TWELVE ARCHANGELS
OF THE CENTRAL SUN

God manifested twelve Angelic Kingdoms from each of the twelve Souls radiating from the center. These twelve kingdoms of energy produce a majestic symphony of Sound and Light and love and they are called the **Twelve Archangels of the Central Sun**. Archangel means "protector of Oneness." We build arches and bridges uniting all physical and nonphysical forms of Creation with each other. We have awareness of all life, and we can feel and communicate with every particle of God's energy.

It is our responsibility to bring Earth and all her children back **home** to the center of Oneness. Our work will be completed when every human thought and feeling returns to the vibration of Divine Love. Mother Father God, in unity with Divine Love and Creation, requested the assistance of the Twelve Archangels in testing the strength and resourcefulness of Oneness. This is where the story of Earth begins.

THE STORY OF
THE BEGINNING OF EARTH

One moment, Father God asked Mother God what it would be like if thought were separate from emotion, and Sound were separate from Light.

What would happen to Divine Love if it were separate from

Creation? Would the Souls inside the stars and planets and their inhabitants forget Oneness? Would they forget where they come from?

How powerful is Divine Love and would it be strong enough to reunite all of God's particles?

Mother God and Father God and Divine Love and Creation decided to answer these questions by conducting an experiment called "the moment of separation from Oneness."

Deep in the heart of God, in the Central Sun, in the Central Soul, God knew this experiment was for the **greatest good** of all particles of energy.

Why?

Mother God (Divine Emotion) knew the experiment would force Divine Love to stretch itself out from the safe center and create new powers of the Central Soul, the powers of compassion, hope, **faith**, and **trust**.

Together, these forces of love bring God's energy back to **truth**, the truth that Oneness is all-loving and all-powerful. Oneness is all there is and all there ever needs to be.

THE ILLUSION OF TIME

All of God's energy exists at one moment, as God's energy cannot be created or destroyed. God's energy exists in the moment, having no past or future, being all there is, and all there ever will be.

The Archangel **Lucifer Michael** carried forth the **will** of God and created the illusion of time. Time is a thought without emotion, without love, and time is the catalyst for inventing separation. Time created the illusion of making two moments, one before and one after.

Mother Father God took a breath in these moments of before and after, and the particles of God's energy appeared to move in a straight line with one before and one behind. The illusion gave the particles temporary amnesia so that they believed they were no longer moving in a spiral. They believed they were disconnected from the center. During this moment of amnesia, Father God (Divine Thought) and Mother God (Divine Emotion) created the illusion of one moment of separation between them and so for one moment, Sound appeared to be separated from Light, and thought was separated from emotion.

A window of time lasting one breath of God was all that Lucifer Michael needed to create the sun Horus, the sun of your solar system, and from Horus, Earth and her brother and sister planets were birthed. Horus and Earth and her brother and sister planets were born in a moment where the illusion of separation from the Center of God appeared to be reality.

After this breath, the window of time was closed, and all the particles of God's energy, the Sound and the Light once again consciously knew they moved in a spiral, and all Souls knew they were connected to the Central Sun.

SPLIT

Lucifer Michael designed Earth as a schoolroom where Souls could come and create a false reality, a reality fully experiencing the illusion of separation from God and from each other. Earth was to be the library for all the Universe and store all learning about Creation and the great **duality** between Oneness and separation.

The sun, Horus, and the other planets and moons were to protect Earth and assist her, and so the science of astrology was invented. Several other star systems as well as Earth's brothers and sisters were designed as training camps for particles of God's energy wishing to participate in the learning process called duality.

During this instant, a mere fraction of a breath for God, the great story of illusion was established, and on the Earth, the Archangel Lucifer Michael appeared to split into two separate Angelic Kingdoms.

Lucifer carried forth the will of God and sent out the illusionary thought, "Separation from God is real," and from separation, fear was born. Michael carried forth the will of God and the human ego was given the power to think thoughts that were not for the greatest good or **highest joy.**

FEAR

Neither Lucifer nor Michael nor any of the other Archangel Kingdoms knew that because fear originated from illusion, it had the fantastic ability to rapidly produce more fear. Soon, fear was casting a spell of forgetting and putting human brains to sleep. Humans began to forget truth, the truth that Oneness is love and love is all there is.

In the beginning of time on Earth, the concept of fear spread slowly because the particles of God's energy making up the human brain remembered Oneness. As time passed, the particles started to forget they were connected to the Central Sun; they began to believe in separation, and Master Fear encouraged them to forget and create more fear.

As fear multiplied, humanity began to feel afraid of humanity, of life itself, and of God. The human mind even separated into the ego mind—the mind believing in fear—and the creative mind—the mind remembering God. For many humans, the ego mind took control. Thus, they began to forget that they are the creators of their reality, and so they were enmeshed more and more in the illusion that separation from God is real and that living life is something to be afraid of.

THE END OF THE EXPERIMENT

As the creative minds of Earth's children began to go silent, so did their abilities to communicate with other particles of God existing on Earth and other planets. They began to believe in the ultimate abandonment by God and lost their awareness of their immortality. When they no longer could communicate with Oneness, the realm of Heaven disappeared and became a separate place for Souls without minds and bodies, a place reachable only through death.

Some members of the human race learned how to quiet the ego

mind and become immune from fearful thoughts. Some of these same people used their remembering to take control over others, giving them the false message that they were capable of something others were not. Entire populations of people gave their minds and bodies over to rulers who threatened them with death or punishment. They gave up the power of knowing that they come from Oneness and are responsible for creating their reality on Earth.

Many Beings of Divine Love came to Earth to teach humanity the truth again, and still fear lulled the human brain back to sleep. Each time fear's illusions caused one human being to harm another, the whole Earth would feel abandoned and alone.

Earth's feelings of desperation were instantly felt deep in the heart of God. Mother Father God, in unity with Divine Love and Creation, decided immediately to end the experiment. God called the Twelve Archangels to intercede and thus began the *divine intervention* of Angels in the daily lives of human beings.

THE LAW OF ONE

Lucifer had watched his work bring rapid destruction to the precious library of Oneness, and so he called on his other half, Michael, to establish the **Law of One** on Earth. This law of Mother Father God, Divine Love, and Creation allows humans to manifest only those experiences that are for the greatest good and learning of all concerned. Humans can still think fearful thoughts, but these thoughts are prevented from destroying Earth. Even if it appears they have great power, the truth is, fear is illusion and fear is not allowed to destroy the **Great School of Duality**.

The knowledge of the Law of One has always lived in the creative mind of every human being, and now is the time for you to remember this law and bring your brain back to an understanding of Oneness. It is now time in Earth time for Heaven and Earth to be reunited and experience only what is for the highest joy and good of all.

THE SPIRAL OF SOUND AND LIGHT

When Lucifer and Michael first split, Michael was given the job of protecting the truth. He did this by creating a door in the creative mind that was always open, a door connecting the creative mind to God's energy of your Soul and your Soul to the Central Soul. Angels call this door your **OverSoul**, or Body of Sound and Light. The key to finding the door is love, remembering to love every particle of your mental, emotional, physical, and spiritual self unconditionally.

Michael brings the truth that each particle of energy in your brain is connected to every particle in every human brain that has lived, is living, or ever will live. As you love yourself and open the door to your creative mind, you assist the opening of all creative minds and of all Souls. When the door is opened, the boundary between Heaven and Earth will dissolve, and humanity will be free to enjoy the great library and consciously be one with all of God.

Lucifer and Michael are now reunited on your planet and, together with all the Archangels of the Central Soul, they are here to teach you how to transform the illusion of fear and separation back to love and Oneness.

It is the will of God for humanity to remember that God is a most magnificent spiral of Sound and Light, a symphony playing joyful music, and you are a most critical instrument in the orchestra.

The Archangels of the Central Sun invite you to experience their guidance to creating **miracles** and coming home to Heaven. We give you tools in abundance to make your journey comfortable and effortless.

 Home

The Archangel of Purest Light and Divine Will asks you to breathe deeply and slowly. Imagine that your entire body is saturated with bright white Light. Change the color to sapphire blue Light. Go back and forth between white and blue until you feel clear and peaceful.

Now, allow the white Light and sapphire Light to blend until you are the color of the sky, a clear Light blue.

Allow your **physical body** to dissolve completely in the Light until you are particles of energy. Say, **"I Am home."** Repeat the word "home" until you experience the euphoria of Oneness.

Book 2

Heaven on Earth

Meeting the Twelve Archangels
of the Central Sun

We call ourselves the Twelve Archangel Kingdoms of the Central Sun or Soul of God. We are like twelve spokes connecting to a great wheel. This great wheel is suspended in a sphere of the Sun's Light, together making the Central Soul, the Center of Oneness, and the Center of the Cosmos.

We can stretch out our spokes of Light and Sound and expand into an infinite number of Angels and fill all the Universe at the same moment. All twelve spokes of God's wheel are saturating Earth with our Light, **music**, power, and healing.

Coming from inside the ball of energy, from each of the twelve spokes, you can hear a beat identical in rhythm to the human heart. Our hearts sing together with yours. When we are invited into your holy space, we fill all your **auras** (energy fields) with our presence and our heartbeat.

When Archangels embrace you, we see, feel, experience, and know everything you do. Once this connection is made, it can never be severed, and you will never be the same again.

Our energy is magical and all-penetrating; it stretches you and makes you demand to know your truth and carry it out courageously. When one of us touches you, you will know all that God knows, and you will again see the total beauty of your planet and of your life.

Angels touch you again and again, and each time, your energy fuses with our energy. With every sensual fusion, you are changed for the highest joy and good of all. We enjoy being your **Guides** and helping you to integrate the spiritual perspective of your life with the mundane.

You are our responsibility, and we are escorting you home to the sanctuary of Divine Love found right inside your own higher self.

Some of your teachers call us Wind, Water, Mineral, Fire, and Ether. To others, our names are Thought, Feeling, Communication, Will, **Manifestation**, Destruction, and Transformation. We call ourselves "Loving-kindness," and we are here to offer you our healing music and energy. We look forward to walking with you and sharing God's wisdom of fully living life on Earth. You are all that we are, one power making up the mind, heart, body, and Soul of Mother Father God.

We welcome you to experience us and find the Heaven you have been waiting for. The words "I Am" mean just this. We ask you to say the words, "I Am one with God" and dance with us here in Heaven. Come, we will talk, and you will understand. Freedom is yours when God lives inside you and you live inside God.

Center of the Wheel

Please breathe in deeply and slowly. Hold your breath for a few moments and then exhale completely. Please continue breathing with deep and slow inhales and exhales.

Imagine you are looking at a very big wheel—made of gold—that is lying on the ground in front of you. The wheel has twelve spokes coming out from a circle in the middle. Please step into the middle of the circle in the middle of the wheel. Say, "Twelve Archangels of the Central Sun, I welcome you into my dream." The wheel will become alive with a rainbow of color and move from the ground to far above your head. You will feel the wheel start to move in a counterclockwise direction. Stay in the vortex of love energy and focus on your breathing. Listen for a message to come to you from the Twelve Archangels. This message will give you insight into where your dream, your reality is changing for your greatest good and highest joy.

It is our mission for God to prove to humanity that Heaven has always existed right inside of you. Heaven is the home of Mother Father God and all your dreams-come-true. Imagine a piece of real estate, a property that belongs to you. You become the caretaker and tend the land and riches and share with all whom you love. Together you live in paradise, trusting in everyone you meet and living life for the greatest good of all. This truth is Mother Father God's intention for you, and now is the time for you to face fear—the thief who stole your estate.

When you give love to this great master of illusion, the master transforms and your wealth of joyous experience expands. Fear is this master, and fear holds humanity in a spell, a spell tied and bound with just one thin cord. The cord holds you completely captive just like a puppet with only one string. Slicing through this cord is a simple feat, and then again moving mountains from one state to another would seem easier to you.

If we teach you how to cut through the cord called fear hanging around your neck, then you join in our mission, and you will be called to go forth and teach others how to find Heaven inside themselves. In no time at all, everyone will know the secret of how to take back their estate, and Heaven will become the only home you know. You will be a true **master**.

We will ask you to remember again and again, it is only one string, not many, only one fear that keeps humanity from living in complete freedom and harmony with Mother Earth. Fear is clever at trying to distract you from this simple truth. Fear breeds complication, chaos, and confusion, and when you confront fear with its own secret, fear loses power over you.

 Slicing the Cord of Master Fear

Please take some deep breaths and exhale completely and inhale deeply. Begin to repeat the phrase, "I Am love."

Please imagine that you are looking at yourself in a full-length mirror. The you that is reflected back has a black velvet ribbon tied around your neck and a second black velvet ribbon tied around your hips. Please reach through the mirror and untie the ribbon around your hips and then untie the ribbon around your neck. In your hand you have a sword ablaze with Archangel Michael's **sapphire blue Flame.** Immediately place this sword into each ribbon. Repeat the exercise until both ribbons have turned into white dust at your feet. Imagine that you sweep the dust out the door using a broom made of gold Light.

THE SECRET

Once upon a distant plane, a place called Heaven existed both day and night. Angels and humans and stars and creatures of all colors and design walked together in peace and harmony.

During a great explosion of Sound and Light, Master Fear arrived in a blast of black smoke. He said to Heaven, "I am really an Angel in disguise, and I have come to teach you what Heaven really is." "You see," he said to all of us, "if you do not experience what it feels like to lose Oneness, then you can never truly know Heaven's grace."

Then Master Fear began his work of stripping Heaven of its bounty, and we all started to sense our foundation breaking underneath our feet. With nothing to stand on, with nothing to rely on, we took on our greatest fear, our fear of abandonment. Abandonment of Mother Father God's love and support, abandonment of Heaven from the plane of Earth, abandonment of Angels' wings of love and protection are fear's greatest illusions.

Black smoke filled the air, the water, and the land with sleeping potion. Everyone fell asleep, sleeping soundly under blankets of illusion. Angel Fires of healing energy appeared to dilute and become incongruent. It appeared that Mother Earth herself had succumbed to death, as even her inhabitants abandoned her.

Smoke is smoke, and now is the moment to clear the smoke screen away. Many of your scholars speak as if the smoke is solid, as if this sleeping potion can have some permanent effect on you. Wake from your sleep, open your eyes, and listen to us carefully, for we are going to tell you how to clear out the smoke.

We are here to show you, Master Fear is an Angel in disguise.

Master Fear's spell is broken when you remember that abandonment is a figment of Master Fear's imagination. The only cure for abandonment is completely filling the human **vessel** with Mother Father God's Divine Love. Receiving love from outside your own self, from other humans, earthly possessions, or from intellectual pursuits does not substitute for Divine Love. Master Fear would like you to believe that love can come only from outside yourself.

We reveal the secret: Divine Love comes from inside, inside your heart where the riches of your Soul, the infinite source of God, lives. We are here to show you the Angel way for opening the source and filling your whole self with ultimate, complete fulfillment. In the process of allowing yourself to receive Divine Love, the human mind, body, emotions, and spirit gradually let go of the fear of abandonment. As the **evolution** continues, life becomes more free and joyful, and eventually your outer reality looks, feels, smells, and tastes like paradise. When your vessel is full and your thirst for love is completely satisfied, then, and only then can you fully enjoy loving and receiving love from other humans, earthly possessions, and intellectual pursuits.

Can you imagine your world when every human being lives in this reality, the reality of Heaven on Earth? What would it be like to live in a world where fear does not exist? We are certain you will join in our mission to cut through the cord holding you captive to Master Fear's illusion.

STEP ONE: FILLING
THE VESSEL WITH DIVINE LOVE

We begin. The first step alternates with the second step. There are only two steps to creating miracles. We will ask you to repeat these two steps until every human being is awake, free, and living in peace and harmony. The process takes one moment. We are certain you are ready!

Filling Up

Go to your kitchen and take a cup from the shelf. Hold it with both hands. The God Essence in you helped to manifest this cup, and this is why it is in your cabinet. Feel the cup and send love to the cup. Allow the cup to represent you as if the cup is you as a small child. Look down on your heart, and feel the heart beat within your chest. Listen to the beat. Imagine an **emerald green** gold Light starting to flow out from your heart, and see the Light of Divine Love fill the cup you are holding.

Now drink the Divine Love from the cup and let it flow into yourself. See the energy flow into every cell of your entire body. Now say, "I Am Divine Love."

Continue to drink Divine Love from your cup; open your imagination and visualize the cup as the child within your heart. Send Divine Love to each other in a rainbow of colors, and say, "I Am God's rainbow of love and I give my love to you."

❖❖❖

STEP TWO: LETTING GO

Step two is allowing God, Divine Love, to come first in your daily life. We have discovered humans have the best intentions at following step two, and then step two gets lost in abandonment all over again. It is the fear of abandonment that tells you constantly to place others, their responsibilities, their issues, and problems and concerns above those of your own heart.

We ask you to sit with this concept for a moment and ask your higher self if this feels like truth.

To move past the fear of abandonment and allow Divine Love to come first, *it is necessary for you to let go of every person, every possession, and every situation or experience you are afraid of losing.* We call this your journey through the hell of your attachments.

Once you have faced the fear of losing what you are attached to, the fear is gone, and you will have the thing, person, situation, or experience returned to you, or something even better.

The Twelve Archangels are leading you through your attachments one step at a time. Often, you do not know what you are attached to until the attachment is taken away. Angels are Grim Reapers in that we take away your fears so you can experience your heart's desires and most miraculous dreams-come-true.

We thank you for bravely choosing to assist us in bringing Heaven and Earth back together.

To take the second step, ask us to show you—gently—what you are attached to through fear. Our promise is that as you let go of all your ego tells you that you must control, true love and eternal freedom will come to you. We remind you, Master Fear is an Angel in disguise. All that Mother Father God requires from you is to face your fears because fear tells your mind not to believe God supplies all you need for your greatest good and evolution. As soon as you become aware of what you are afraid of losing, surrender the fear and know once you face it, the fear no longer exists.

Here is an example of a common human fear: one day, you discover you have an attachment to money. Angels will hold your hands and support you as you travel through the experience of having no money or, to be more accurate, having no money when you expect to have the money. We will help you let go of believing you must have money to survive, and we will help you show yourself that you do not need to compromise your integrity to obtain money.

At the moment of your complete surrender, money will come. The entire experience can take an instant, and when you *allow our assistance,* the experience of releasing the attachment can be effortless and painless.

Letting go is a process, and often attachments hide other attachments. When you ask for our guidance, we will show you how to peel through the attachments at Light speed. Keep breathing, close your eyes, hang on tight, and repeat step one. Before you know it, you will have more of what your heart wants than you have ever dreamed of, and better yet, you will not be afraid of losing it.

❀ Letting Go

Breathe out, like you are blowing out the candles on your birthday cake. Breathe in, a nice deep breath, and say "ahhh" on the exhale. Repeat breathing in, nice and slow, and saying, "ahhh" on the exhale.

See yourself holding a book. The book is called "Expectations for My Future." You are standing on a bridge overlooking a winding river. The water in the river is radiant white and gold. Drop the book into the river and say, "I surrender. I let go."

Repeat dropping the book into the river and saying, "I surrender. I let go," until you feel very brave.

Take a deep breath and jump into the river.

This is the River of Trust. It is like no other river. Be the colors of the river; and feel the river move inside of you, as you move inside the river. Say again, "I surrender. I let go."

Return to step one, and fill your vessel with Divine Love.

❖❖❖

Following step one and step two will make your human consciousness expand. As you fill your vessel, it overflows with Divine Love, and with Divine Love comes Divine power.

If you follow our two steps, we give you our 100 percent guarantee that soon you will have Heaven all around you, and you will know you are equal in love power to an Archangel.

For Heaven to return, we need *you!* Everyone is called, and the more who come, the faster the will of God will be done on Earth as it is in Heaven.

To know what an Angel knows, sees, and feels, and to perform healing miracles like an Angel can do, follow step one and step two.

Blessings and thank God for *you.*

Book 3

Angel Power

Working with the God Force of the Chakras

Human beings have all the magic they need to create miracles every moment of their existence on Earth. Mother Father God's miraculous power is available to you through the batteries of spiritual energy found within your **spiritual body**. Your spiritual body is much bigger than your physical body. It is so large that you cannot see all of it with your human eyes. Your spiritual body is filled with energy centers or **chakras**. Some of these chakras are located within the boundary of your physical body as well as above and below it. When these chakras are open, all of this miraculous God power is available for you to use to facilitate miracles.

Miracles are gifts of Mother Father God's **divine grace**. They happen in the moment and always when you need them for your highest joy and greatest good. As you open your mind and become more aware of what your spiritual experiences are showing you about your divine self, you might begin to discover miracles happening all the time. Miracles require trust in God's divine plan.

When you ask God for a miracle, know God always comes through in God's time and in God's way. Angels specialize in seeing the big picture. We can see how manifesting your request affects all of human-ity. Often, we are called to orchestrate and synchronize miracles so all God's Creation benefits from each gift of divine grace.

Angel power, intention, imagery, and affirmations are used for open-ing your awareness to perceive God's incredible, amazing magic happen-ing for you exactly when you need it most. Our power comes in handy for helping those you love *and* those you dislike. Working with Angel power follows God's laws. Our power can only be used for the greatest good of all. We invite you to work with our Angelic healing energies and use your imagination to invent new ways for waking up humanity. Every human being has equal potential for opening and receiving the infinite love and abundant wealth of the Universe. All people can live in peace, plenty, good health, and continuous joy.

We, the Twelve Archangels of the Central Sun, will show you how!

CONNECTING WITH
THE ANGEL POWER OF THE CHAKRAS

Learning to use Angel power begins with asking for our assistance. We work together to uphold your vibration so your higher self can open the vaults of healing energies held within your chakras. The chakras belong to the spiritual body and you can access them through seeing the colors. Your job is to visualize the color of the chakra whose vibra-tion matches what you need. Please note that we present you with the chakras in the order that you need to *open* them. This order is not the typical order that you will find in a book on chakras. Angels use a slightly different variation of the color than human teachers use. Our colors work as *healing* vibrations and therefore may be softer than expected.

The list below is an overview of the chakras and other important energy centers, including their locations, colors, and uses. More in-depth guided imagery exercises follow this list. Notice if you are drawn to any specific chakra, and continue to explore it in the exercises.

1. **Third eye chakra.** Also called the "eye of God." Located around and in the area of your forehead, extending to the back of your head and covering the tips of your ears. **Fuchsia with an indigo center.** This chakra is the power source for your intuition channel and connects your spiritual body to the conscious thoughts and images of your **mental body.**

2. **Crown chakra.** Located at the very top of the head. Royal purple (or a soft shade of lavender for infants and young children). The healing energy connects with your higher self; your higher self always stays in Heaven and governs the creative and spiritual spaces within your mind. Home to the violet Flame of transformation and forgiveness.

3. **Root chakra.** Located around the tailbone at the base of the spine. Clear ruby pink. Home to Divine Mother's **Holy Spirit**; the healing energy of the root chakra works to clear negative and blocked emotion, heal physical illness, and supports receiving abundance from the Universe.

4. **Will chakra.** Located in and around the throat. Sapphire blue. Home to Archangel **Michael's Flame** of truth, courage, awareness, and justice, the healing energy of the will chakra is masculine and active. It supports the surrendering of the ego to the Soul's direction.

5. **Heart chakra.** Located in the heart area. Emerald green, with a pure, sweet sound that accompanies it. The healing energy of the heart chakra works to fill the mind and vessel with unconditional love.

6. **Turquoise Flame or Light.** The combination of the heart and will chakras. Any shade of turquoise or aqua, with gold sparkles. The Angel power of the turquoise Flame supports dreaming and the manifestation of hopes and dreams.

7. **Solar plexus chakra.** Located just below the ribcage, expanding far beyond the physical body. The bright, golden Light of the sun. The healing energy of this chakra supports the positive

expression of personal power, confidence, and the attracting of positive attention from others.

8. **Soul chakra.** Located about navel level, covering the reproductive organs. Rich sunset colors, soft and bright corals, orange, ruby pink (these colors may remind you of a well-fueled bonfire). The Soul chakra is the receptacle for the energy coming in from the higher self, or OverSoul. Home to the coral orange Flame of creativity, passion, and fuel for the Soul's attraction power.

9. **White Fire.** Originates outside of the human vessel, in your OverSoul. To use this Angel power, use your intention and ask us to put what you desire to protect in a white Fire diamond. We call this the Angel Fire of protection and purification.

Angel power is *powerful*. These healing energies facilitate change for the better. When a human being is hurt, it is natural instinct to want to hurt back. Using Angel power actually raises the instinctual and very low vibration of violence into the high vibration of positive and correct action. The auras are cleared instantly, and usually the participant is left feeling peaceful with new clarity and forgiveness.

ANGEL POWER VISUALIZATIONS FOR TRANSFORMATION AND HEALING

Third Eye Chakra: Intuition

The third eye chakra is the power source for your intuition channel, connecting your spiritual body to the conscious thoughts and images of your mental body. The more you use the healing power of this chakra, the more available and clearer your intuitive voice becomes to your conscious thinking. For this exercise, do invite God's Child, the child within your heart, to join you in the communication.

Working with the Fuchsia and Indigo Flame

Imagine that you place a fuchsia miner's lamp on your head. The light on the lamp sits in the middle of your forehead. A deep indigo blue cave appears in front of you. Please enter the cave and listen for the soft sounds of a flowing stream. Ask the Goddess of Intuition to take your hands and guide you deeper into her home in order to turn on the lights in the cave. Say, "Light of my intuitive truth, guide me to know, see, feel, and hear." When the gold and pink Lights turn on, ask the Goddess for help with any challenging decisions that you need to make. Be sure to thank her.

Crown Chakra:
Transformation and Forgiveness

The crown chakra's **violet Fire**, Light, or transforming energy is responsible for clearing your mental body of anxiety and negative thoughts or thoughts of low vibration. Violet Fire is extremely thorough at erasing fear and changing fear back into love. Here are some methods for activating and using violet Fire.

 Violet Fire Rain Shower for
Transforming Painful Memories

The subconscious holds onto painful memories like a sponge. The little child within you knows all about these memories. Ask him to show you any scene from the past that needs to be transformed into something much happier.

Close your eyes. See yourself, and your wounded child self, standing in a lush tropical forest. Vibrant flowers of every hue surround you. Soft violet and gold raindrops begin to fall on your heads and form a puddle at your feet. You carry photos of painful moments from your childhood. Drop them into the violet, golden puddles and see the scenes change from hurting to tender. As they shift, you move from distress to feeling untroubled. Put sorrows and fears into the puddles of violet Fire and say, "I let go of the past and all that disappointed me. I forgive myself, and all who have hurt me. I am free to begin my new life, full of Heaven's abundance, today!"

◇◇◇

 Violet Fire Nectar for Anxiety

The ego self can easily feel afraid or defensive when he or she feels out of control. Anxiety, a physical and emotional panic response to feeling out of control, needs to be short-circuited so that you can function and make choices that are for your greatest good.

Close your eyes and imagine that the air you breathe is a soft lavender color. Continue to breathe in the pure lavender oxygen and ask the shaman of the rain forest for some violet Fire nectar. The shaman in the forest will come and offer you a cup that looks like a large purple blossom. Drink the purple nectar in the cup. It will taste sweet and refreshing. Say, "Thank you, Peace, that you have found me." Continue to breathe in the lavender air and repeat, "Thank you, Peace, that you have found me," until you feel clear and calm.

◇◇◇

 Violet Fire Rebirthing

Violet Fire works splendidly for situations requiring release, forgiveness, and rebirth.

Close your eyes. See yourself wading out into a gently flowing violet river. Next to you is a camel carrying all of your baggage. Your luggage is filled with emotional pain and loss from the past, and fears concerning the future. Perched high on your luggage is your briefcase containing all of the documentation on why you need to hold onto your resentments and victim consciousness. Take the heavy briefcase of burdens and throw it into the flowing violet river. Invite your camel to join you. Unload your luggage and send it down river. Say, "I release all of my burdens, fears, and sorrows to the violet Fire of transformation and forgiveness." Take a peaceful swim in the river until you dissolve completely in the violet color. Say, "I Am now reborn into a new and better life."

 ### Violet Fire Waterfall for Regular Clearing

Close your eyes and see that you are standing under a violet Fire waterfall. Take slow, deep breaths and visualize the negative commentary in your mind as dried mud stuck to your hair and skin. Wash the negative thoughts and fears away in the violet Fire water. Say, "I surrender. I choose *love*," again and again until you feel joyful.

 ### Violet Fire Swimming Pool for Clearing Negativity

Swimming in a pool filled with violet Fire water is nurturing and healing for your human Soul. In this **visualization**, do not be afraid if the water of the pool turns dark. The water may turn dark when you have absorbed negativity or fear from other people or from an environment (such as hospital, restaurant, or crowded venue).

Close your eyes and jump into a swimming pool of beautiful purple Light. Know that all the negativity you have absorbed is being transmuted and neutralized. See yourself as a sponge and invite your **Guardian Angels** to wring out any darkness. Expand in the violet water of Light and step out of the swimming pool, clear, open and refreshed.

Violet Fire Hat for Erasing Self-doubt and Mental Confusion

When you visualize a violet Fire hat on your head, you will discover that your worries and self-doubt are erased from your conscious thoughts. The hat works by opening up your own crown chakra and filling your brain cells with God's Divine Love in the form of crystal clear Divine Thought. Because you cannot think from a position of love and fear at the same moment, fear is cleared away.

This Angel hat works extremely well for calming obsessive thinking about the future. We recommend that students wear their hat for all exams, presentations, and interview situations because when you are thinking clearly, you can create a joyful learning experience. Wearing the hat helps your brain to open so you can retrieve—from the Universe or from your own memory banks—what you need.

> Close your eyes. See yourself designing a stylish violet hat for you to wear. It can be tall or short, eloborate or plain. Do make sure it covers your forehead and your ears. Imagine that you dance around in your hat to make sure that it stays on your head. Focus your mind's eye on the color violet!

Violet Fire Eraser and Magic Blackboard for Erasing Limiting Beliefs

Stored within your subconscious are old concepts and beliefs about yourself, humanity, and reality that need to be transformed. For example, you or someone in your family may hold the belief that other family members are destined to experience hardship on the Earth. Perhaps because your mother died of cancer, you have a buried belief that you may be diagnosed with cancer. The mind likes to make connections between experiences in the past and expectations for the future. The magic, violet Light blackboard works to show you how your subconscious beliefs are manifesting problems for you today. The blackboard also works to illuminate how these beliefs are predicting events in the future.

When you write something on this mental blackboard, your higher mind draws an equation for you connecting what you believe to be true in your subconscious with the reality you are currently experiencing. Remember, your thoughts manifest your reality. It is very helpful to erase limiting beliefs *before* they manifest a crisis in your life. Likewise, if a crisis is happening in your life, write down the crisis on the magic blackboard and watch your higher mind show you the belief in your subconscious that is manifesting the crisis. Here is an example: Let's say that you are experiencing financial lack. Write this down on the violet Light blackboard. You will see that your higher mind turns this into an equation where lack equals *unworthiness*. Now, erase the equation: *lack = unworthiness* and watch your higher mind give you a new belief in your mind. In our example, you will see: *abundance = worthy of love*.

Take a deep breath and blow out. Do this three times. Write something on the magic blackboard that is causing you to suffer. Ask your higher mind to fill out the equation for you. Erase the equation with a violet Fire eraser and say, "I forgive." Your higher mind will give you a new belief equation. If this belief is still not satisfactory, repeat the exercise. Now, write your name on the magic blackboard. Watch as your higher mind fills out the equation of what you are expecting for yourself in the future. Erase anything that you don't like. Your higher mind will continue to give you a new belief, at a higher vibration, with every new equation that you erase from your subconscious. The goal of using the magic blackboard is to attain an equation such as: *Living life on Earth = Living life in Heaven.* Open your eyes and state your new belief to yourself.

Root Chakra: Divine Mother's Unconditional Love and Compassion

The **ruby Flame**, or Holy Spirit, is Mother God's unconditional love energy of pure emotion. This energy is supplied to you from your root chakra located at the base of your spine. This energy center grounds you to Mother Earth so you can receive all the material resources you need to live on Earth in a healthy body. When this chakra is open and fully functioning, the human being is not afraid of abandonment.

Working with the root chakra Angel power allows you to clear away blocked emotion, insecurity, and low self-esteem. Mother God's love is soothing and nurturing. Her love is essential for healing the little child inside your heart. Working with the ruby Flame will bring you peace of mind and relaxation to your body. The unconditional love of Mother God merged with the abundant love from Mother Earth creates an experience you can feel with your physical body as well as your emotional and mental bodies.

 Ruby Flame Healing Soak

Breathe in deeply and exhale slowly. Repeat until you feel calm. See yourself and the child of your heart joyfully playing in the ruby mineral springs. Soak up the rich ruby Light of Divine Mother's love, and allow all your stress from the day to melt away. Say, "I Am open to receiving all I need from the Universe. I Am filling up with Divine Mother's love."

 Ruby Pink Angel Blanket for Dissipating Anger

Angel blankets gently calm down the most savage temper. We invite you to wrap yourself or someone you know who needs calming affection in a ruby pink Angel blanket of unconditional love.

See yourself resting peacefully underneath a soft ruby blanket of Light. Please breathe in the nurturing comfort of the energy. Say, "I Am safe and secure."

◈◈◈

 ## Scarlet Red Fire Dragon for Releasing Anger

Imagine that you are a great red dragon. Feel the strength of your mighty claws and wings. Allow yourself to feel your anger. Your dragon breath is made of violet Fire. Breathe your violet Fire on the situation that is causing you to feel powerless and trapped. Say, "I transform the energy of my anger into clarity of purpose. I choose to change my reality by changing myself."

◈◈◈

 ## Drinking from the Cup of Divine Love

The cup of Divine Love is a sacred bowl made of gold Light that is filled with ruby pink Divine Mother's love. This ruby Light vibrates at a special frequency, as it shares both Mother God's unconditional love and Divine Love's deep healing power of Soul.

If you are a healer of others, we hope you will bring your patients to this healing sanctuary. You need never fear you are trespassing another's boundaries by visualizing others in Holy Spirit. If it is for their greatest good, their own OverSoul hears your request and brings them to the sanctuary. You are acting as a messenger from a place of love and compassion.

See any hurting, sexually or physically abused aspects of yourself diving into the Great Golden Cup. As you move through the Light, know that every particle of God's energy that is you is cleansed and made new. Every atom of your physical, mental, and **emotional body** is recreated and cleared of all trauma your vessel is ready to release. Drink from the cup and visualize the ruby energy filling every cell of your body, restoring you and healing you of the loss from the past.

◈◈◈

Riding the Red Horse of
Emotional Power for Removing Emotional Blocks

Mother God's energy of emotion can work like dynamite to blast open blockages preventing your whole self from feeling your feelings and from understanding what your feelings are telling you. Remember, feelings are actually mental messages identifying where emotional energy is blocked in your vessel. When it benefits your growth to know how the blocks were created, you will remember. If it is not for your greatest good to remember, the blockage is cleared without engaging your conscious awareness.

Riding a beautiful scarlet horse, the "Red Horse of Emotion," is an extremely powerful visualization experience that has the potential to greatly free your emotional body. **Divine law** allows you to visualize only yourself riding the Red Horse because if you have the desire, then your consciousness is ready. This is not a decision you are allowed to make for another human being.

> Close your eyes, breathe in deeply, and exhale slowly until you feel centered. Say, "I Am calling the Red Horse to me now." See yourself climb up on the horse's back. Hang on tight and make any sound you like. The Red Horse knows how long a ride you are ready for; when the ride is complete, you will find yourself fully awake, present, and aware of your surroundings.

❖❖❖

Will Chakra: Truth, Courage, and Awareness

The power of God's will and truth comes from the energy center located in the throat area. When this energy center is open, your conscious awareness is connected with your heart, and you are living your purest truth and communicating this truth in thoughts, words, and actions. The sapphire blue Flame of truth gives your ego the courage to surrender its free will to the highest will of God. Surrendering the will of ego opens you to know your real truth, speak from your God center, and act for the greatest good of all.

Working with Archangel Michael's Fire helps you clear out all the times in your life where you have swallowed your positive willpower and repressed speaking your truth. Become united with the will of God, and live your life on Earth awake and active instead of passive and resistant! Archangel Michael's Flame of truth lights the way to higher self-expression and freedom for all who have the courage to live their truth!

Anointed by Archangel Michael's Sword of Truth

Placing Michael's sword of God's will in your spinal column sends the message to your whole vessel and to all God's Creation that you are ready and willing to receive your freedom and to experience your greatest heavenly destiny here on Earth.

> Close your eyes, and center your vessel by breathing in deeply and exhaling slowly. Invite Archangel Michael to place his sword of sapphire blue Flame into the top of your head, all the way down your spine, filling your backbone with sapphire blue Light. The Light of God's will is anchored into the ground beneath your feet. Say, "I Am willing to know my truth, see my truth, hear my truth, speak my truth, and live my truth according to God's will for the highest joy and greatest good of all."

◈◈◈

Blue Fire Arrows of Truth for Addiction

When a human being is struggling with addiction, it is truth that will set you free. All addictions happen when individuals are in denial of their real power and potential. This denial may be a response to emotional suffering in childhood or during life. When the reality of everyday life is overwhelming, there is a better choice than becoming dependent on a chemical or unhealthy practice. We offer you a method that can help you or someone you love break free of the lies that are the root cause of the addictive behavior.

For yourself:

Ask Archangel Michael to shoot a flaming blue Light arrow into your head and another arrow into your heart. See the blue Light fill your mind, then see the blue Light fill your heart. Now, see the blue Light fill your entire body and expand out from your body. Change the color to gold and see gold Light filling you. Say, "I Am reclaiming my power and living my truth. I surrender my past choices to my higher will. I Am choosing to make healthy choices for myself and live a new life." The words "I Am" call on the power of your OverSoul to help you see God's truth in your life.

For someone else:

See yourself shoot the arrows into their root and Soul chakra as well as their head and heart. Say, "I call on God's will in action. I ask your OverSoul to set you free from the lies that haunt you."

Heart Chakra: Healing and Love

Giving and receiving love in balance and harmony supports the wounded child inside your heart to heal from any past misconceptions or future disillusionments. Opening the heart chakra is a continuous process and will continue forever like an eternal drumbeat. Mother Father God's heart beats with yours, expanding and loving and creating. You were born with the potential for sharing great love with your fellow human beings, and now is the time to achieve this potential for giving and receiving love. As you open your heart, humanity opens, and God's Divine Love pours in, fusing together Heaven and Earth. You are never too old to learn how to receive love, and you are always young enough to give love.

Resting on the Emerald Green Field of Moss

For your heart to open to give love to yourself and to others, it is essential for you to receive love. The imagery of the green Light blanket of moss helps you to experience receiving love from Mother Earth united with the central heart of God. Human beings cannot survive without love, and they need to receive love from Mother Earth to feel connected to God, and to feel connected to their own center.

> See yourself resting on a soft and sweet bed of emerald green moss. The sky above is clear and sunny. The **white gold Light** of Divine Love is flowing over you and into you, filling every cell of your body. At the same time, you are receiving the green Light from Mother Earth's heart chakra flowing into your back and also filling every cell of your body. Say, "I Am receiving healing emerald green heart love into my whole vessel."

 ## Visiting with the God Child within and Dancing with Your Guardian Angels

Your heart chakra is the place inside where you can connect to Heaven at any moment.

> See yourself standing in a sunny emerald green forest, and welcome your **God Child** to come and tell you words of wisdom. This all-knowing child of your heart is happy to bring you your Angels, and together you can solve the problems of the world. The God Child can tell you where love needs to be sent and where you need to allow gentleness into your earthly experiences. See yourself and this magical child dance in the beautiful forest. Invite your Angels to join in the fun. Say, "I Am happy. I Am grateful for my God Child and I Am grateful for my Angels."

Turquoise Flame: Dreams Come True

The Angel power of the turquoise Flame or Light, the fusion of the heart and will chakras, is the manifesting energy that helps dreams come to fruition.

 ### *Visualization for Working with the Turquoise Flame*

Is there a desire that you wish to manifest? A goal that you are dreaming to achieve? Place it in the color turquoise and then invite the turquoise energy, together with the gold energy of Divine Love, to fill every cell of your vessel. Say, "I give thanks for my success!"

Solar Plexus Chakra: Power and Confidence

The solar plexus chakra is located around your stomach area. This energy center is the supplier of your personal power and self-confidence. When you are "hit" by fear, anxiety, or negativity, you may feel sick to your stomach or experience pain and gas. The solar plexus chakra explodes and releases yellow-gold Light of Power whenever you feel insulted, cheated, taken for granted, or criticized.

 ### *Solar Plexus Recharging for Healing from Disrespect*

See yourself swallowing orbs of golden Central Sunlight. See the power go straight to your stomach. Expand the golden Light, bright as the sun, until you are completely filled with the Light. Say, "I allow my Angels to fill me with **respect** and confidence. I choose to use my power for the greatest good of all."

 ### *OverSoul Power Recharge*

Yellow gold Light comes from your own OverSoul; this is the best energy for rebuilding your strength after too much work of any kind.

Imagine yourself resting comfortably on a beautiful beach inside a vast gold sphere of Light. Say, "I Am one with my OverSoul, my higher self." See yourself within this ball of golden Light floating down a yellow river to the white-gold sea of Divine Love. Breathe and relax. Enjoy!

Soul Chakra: Creative Energy

The Soul chakra is the energy center for your sexual energy, creative energy, and the home of your Soul in the human vessel. This chakra is located in and around the area of your navel. Unworthiness attacks this chakra with ruthless attention, for here exists the umbilical cord between Earth and Heaven. The Twelve Archangels of the Central Soul focus much love and attention on humanity's Soul chakra.

 ### *Self-esteem Clean Out*

When the Soul chakra is filled with fear's distortion, the human self can feel deep unworthiness. No list of achievements can ease the discomfort of not feeling good enough.

> See yourself and all your Angels, including the **Nature Angel** of your vessel, assisting you in vacuuming up all the broken pieces of your self-esteem with a violet Fire vacuum cleaner. Use the vacuum cleaner to clear any distorted sexual energy that could look like swarming snakes or insects. Vacuum up all darkness. Breathe, and keep cleaning until you see a soft **coral or orange Light,** like a beautiful sunset, appear and expand out. Say, "I thank myself, my Soul and my Angels for returning worthiness and self-respect to my vessel and to my life."

 ### *Opening the Soul's Treasury of Creative Power*

Imagine that you are together with your Divine Child, Divine Feminine, and Divine Masculine. You are swimming in a coral sea of Light.

Breathe in the Light and see it fill the Universe. An Angel will appear and hand you a small treasure chest. Open it and read what is written on the paper inside. This is a creative idea from your Soul's treasury, given to you by your OverSoul, to create something wonderful for yourself and for humanity. Say, "I Am grateful for my creative power. I allow myself to express this power for my highest joy and greatest abundance."

White Fire: Purification and Protection

The white Fire or Light of your OverSoul chakra creates a protective energy field for you when you are traveling through intense negativity or stressful encounters with others. Shining this Light onto situations and dreams where there is confusion can bring instant clarity. White Light is the energy that purifies any illusion so you can *see* the truth of what is really happening.

With a little practice, you will be amazed at what you can discover working with the Angel power of white Light.

 ### *White Light for Dream Intepretation*

Putting a scene from a nighttime dream or a confusing experience from your daytime life in white Light can show you what you need to learn about what you are manifesting. Earth is where human beings identify where they get caught in fear's illusions. By piercing through the illusion, you can transform the fear and manifest a much happier experience.

For a confusing experience:

Imagine that you are sitting in a movie theater watching the scene of a confusing event from your daytime reality. See white Light flood the images in your movie so that all you see is white Fire. Pay attention to what now appears on the movie screen. What truth has been revealed to you? If you are still confused, ask your Angels to help you understand the new images. Breathe out and relax.

For a nighttime dream:

Flood the scene from your dream in white Light. See what changes in the scene and how this makes you feel. Shine the white Light on anyone in your dream and ask the white Light to reveal the aspect of yourself that you need to transform. Fill this aspect of yourself with violet Light and say, "I forgive and I transform." Is there an animal in your dream? An animal represents a strong feeling. Please talk to the animal and ask it, "What am I feeling? What do I desire?" Continue to work with the white Light until you fully comprehend each piece of your dream. When you feel complete, breathe out deeply, say, "ahhh," and relax.

Angel power works especially well with your intention to set yourself free from fear so that you can experience your **divine destiny**. Together, we will use Mother Father God's love to change reality for the greatest good of all people. Together, we will make rapid progress in bringing Heaven and Earth together.

Angel power helps you to live free at last—we celebrate with you!

Book 4

Light and Dark

Where Does Separation Begin and End?

Mother Father God created you, the human vessel, as a whole being of spirit, thought, emotion, and body. Each vessel is designed to live in complete Oneness with all other vessels and all of Mother Father God's Creation. Inside the human vessel are the four aspects of God:

> Divine Love/spiritual body
> Father/mental body
> Mother/emotional body
> Creation/physical body.

Each aspect or body of the vessel is created to be inseparable from the other. When the bodies are in balance and anchored in God's Sound and Light, the vessel, the human self can experience only a reality of Heaven, perfect joy, peace, harmony, and Oneness. Because your human vessel is one with all other human vessels, when your bodies are completely balanced, you create an infinitely powerful force of Divine Love that pulls all other vessels into balance.

Fear creates a disturbance in the mental body, causing an illusionary perception of separation between the mental, emotional, physical, and spiritual bodies. When your mental body is free of fear, your four bodies will return to their natural state of balance. As you do this continously, all of humanity is supported in returning to a divine state of freedom and inner wholeness.

We, the Twelve Archangel Kingdoms of the Central Sun, welcome you to experience an integration of your thought and feeling, your mind with your spirit and body, as you have never considered to be possible here on Earth. We ask you to find your courage and know as you choose to walk through fear's illusions into Divine Love, you open doorway after doorway for all whom you love.

We tell you a mystery, and we hope perhaps you will be the one to accept the miracle of courage. In truth, to bring Heaven and Earth together in divine union takes only one human vessel. We need one human being brave enough to fight for freedom for your entire human race. You see, bright **Child of God**, Master Fear has tricked you into believing the journey is impossible, that you do not have the strength or the willpower to set your vessel free. We know how wise you are becoming, and so we ask you to walk together with us. We will take you home, and you will never feel alone again.

We begin by describing to you the different parts of the human vessel, and we will tell you how separation between the human and Mother Father God is perpetuated with each part. We will teach you how to heal the separation by reaching deeper and deeper into your Light; as you transform and become one with God consciously, you help all humanity awaken to Heaven.

Heaven is the home of God, and the home of God is found inside your loving heart. We thank you for bringing Heaven and Earth together. We thank you for creating miracles for yourself and those you love.

THE SPIRITUAL BODY

The spiritual body is your **body of Light and Sound**. This energy body holds the human Soul, God's energy existing on the physical Earth dimension, together with the OverSoul, God's energy existing in the dimensions of Heaven. Perhaps you can imagine your spiritual body as the embryonic sac surrounding and nurturing your whole vessel. The sac feeds you with God's Light and Sound as your mental, emotional, and physical self expands, evolves, and rebalances back to a state of Oneness.

The spiritual body provides God's energy to you through the chakras, the energy centers of the human vessel (see Book 3). These energy centers supply Divine Love to all the parts of your physical body as well as give support to your mental body and to your emotional body. Held within the chakras is the memory of all your experiences on Earth in this life or any life, past or future, as well as lives you are living simultaneously but in other worlds of the Universe. You have the ability to communicate with your chakras through your intuition at all times. Intuition is the channel between your spiritual body and your mental body. The body of Sound and Light is constantly sending you messages through the subtle thoughts of your intuitive mind. We are willing to teach you how to hear the voice of your intuition by opening and transforming your mental body. When the thinking mind is clear, you will hear your intuitive thoughts and know they are God's truth.

THE MENTAL BODY

The mental body is your thinking mind, all the multitude of thoughts passing through your brain at any given moment. Some thoughts catch your attention, and you consciously hear their message. Other thoughts drift by and stay in the background, so quiet or buried you may miss their messages entirely. Thoughts are messengers between the mental, spiritual, emotional, and physical bodies.

The mind is similar to a television with the ability to receive a variety of different stations or channels. When the mind's TV is turned on, you can listen and see the current program running through your consciousness. You can think of the TV as your conscious awareness, thoughts you are paying attention to. Your mental TV set can have many stations, yet the viewer typically watches one station or channel at a time.

For you to "tune into" your physical self, your mind turns to the physical body channel on the TV. When you wish to understand the depth of your emotions, the mind selects the appropriate channel for your emotional body. A channel requiring special reception on the TV is the intuition channel, which relays programs from your spiritual body. Angels use the intuition channel to communicate with you. As you open to receiving our love, it becomes easier for you to tune your mental TV to your intuitive thoughts. Intuitive thoughts coming from your spiritual body broadcast news and information giving clarity and insight into your mental, emotional, and physical bodies as well as news concerning other human beings and God's Creation.

Intuitive thought is pure, simple, and quiet compared with the authoritative distracting thoughts of the ego. Angels describe the human ego as your personality. The ego decides how you identify yourself in the world in relation to other people. A free and integrated ego defers authority to the intuition. When this great union between the conscious awareness and intuition happens, the human knows and trusts he or she is a Child of God and worthy of total freedom.

We are here to help you guide your ego back to a place of unity with your spiritual self. To do this, you need to transform all conscious thoughts sending the message you are still separate or unworthy. Fear tells the ego through conscious and subconscious thought patterns to believe only the practical, rational, and tangible.

We wish to describe four important thought patterns generated by fear that enable the ego to stay apart from your spiritual self and the intuitive voice. These thought patterns keep fear alive in your mental, emotional, and physical bodies.

Wanting. "Wanting" thoughts constantly tell you what you want that you do not have in the time and space your ego demands.

Controlling. "Controlling" thoughts suggest what action you must force from yourself or another to get what your ego wants when and where it wants it.

Comparing. "Comparing" thoughts tell you to compare your earthly accomplishments, physical beauty, emotional status, and mental intelligence with other human beings. Comparing thoughts place your ego in competition with all other egos.

Judging. Last are the "judging" thoughts. Judging thoughts often follow comparing thoughts. They evaluate where you are according to the ego's list of standards and expectations for your progress through life.

We will show you how to transform these thought patterns by clearing your mental body with Mother Father God's Divine Love. Fearful thought patterns must be cleared again and again until the mind no longer reacts to them. As the conscious thoughts are cleared, the subconscious thoughts and memories from your past surface and clear. During this cyclical process, the deep subconscious transforms into an instinctual state of trust and unity with all of God's Creation.

The deep subconscious includes concepts you live by that you have no memory of; it is just what you have always done and have always believed about yourself, life, your world, and your relationship to God. As transformation of fearful thought patterns proceeds, the human mind develops and begins to believe miracles are possible, and the ego is integrated with your heart. When the ego and the intuitive voice of your heart become one voice, your conscious awareness is always and forever tuned into your purest truth. God's love and power become the deep subconscious mind, and trusting God's plan becomes a way of life.

Because each human mind is influenced by all other minds, your transformation is connected to the transformation of all other people.

As your mind becomes free, you help all human beings break free from the bonds of Master Fear's slavery. It is only a moment away when all human minds will complement and work synergistically together. Your integrated ego will allow God's purpose for you and all you know to manifest on Earth. Believe that you deserve to live in a world where each human being feels completely satisfied and works in harmony with all living creatures.

Do the following exercise when your mind is obsessing over the future or when negative thoughts are permeating your awareness.

Clearing the Mental Body of Wanting, Controlling, Comparing, and Judging Thought Patterns

We ask you to remember you are welcome to change the imagery. Our visualizations are all metaphorical in that all Angel Fire is a pure vibration of Divine Love. You are holding Archangel Michael's sword of sapphire blue Fire. This is the Light of truth and God's will. Take the sword and quickly slice off your head at the base of your neck. Imagine your head lands gently into a boiling pot of violet Fire, God's energy of transformation and forgiveness. If you prefer, step under a sapphire blue Light waterfall and then a violet Light waterfall, and go back and forth between the two colors until your mind is open and clear. Breathe and say, "I Am love." Do this when your mind is obsessing over the future or when negative thoughts are traveling through your awareness.

◇◇◇

THE EMOTIONAL BODY

Emotion, when allowed to flow free and pure, is Mother God's Holy Spirit. Holy Spirit is unconditional love, the almighty healing force, and cure for all human dysfunction. Feelings are messages generated by the mental body identifying where emotion is blocked or moving freely within the vessel. Joy is a manifestation of feeling Holy Spirit freely within the human self. Sadness, guilt, depression, loneliness, and holding your breath are messages telling you to clear more anger.

Anger is blocked Holy Spirit. When the mind identifies the feeling of anger, the vessel breathes and releases the anger and unlocks the force of emotion to open and heal the heart, mind, and body. Angels see anger as a most positive feeling, for it is anger that can show you the door to freedom. At the primal level, human beings are angry that Mother Father God abandoned them. Clearing anger from your vessel opens the river of Divine Love in your heart. Love flows into your awareness thought by thought and experience by experience, and transforms fear wherever love finds it.

You ask us about the feeling called "fear." We tell you, humans can *think* fear, and you can experience the results of this thought; however, it is impossible for you to experience fear as an emotion. When the mind—whether in the deep subconscious, subconscious, or conscious state—releases or produces fearful thoughts, the heart closes, the Holy Spirit is blocked, and the physical body responds by some form of trauma. This shock can be felt as numbness, pain, or panic. When you remember with your whole mind that nothing in your world can create or destroy you, for you are God's energy, you are free from fear.

As you become free from fear, the Holy Spirit, Mother God's pure unconditional love, fills your inner and outer world, and it is no longer possible for you and the human family to experience fear. Listen to your feelings from your center with your intuitive mind, for these intuitive thoughts will tell you where you still block the Holy Spirit. Opening your heart and centering your mind allows emotion to flow. Allowing yourself to feel your emotion, quietly and privately in your own sacred space, will heal you completely and bring you back to Oneness.

Clearing the Emotional Body

See yourself sitting in a large, round room with the lights off. Turn on the lights and look for any images that make you feel uncomfortable. We have observed many humans finding monsters, weapons, dark

clouds, dying people, hissing snakes, and barbed wire in their emotional space. Visualize a shower of brilliant violet Fire pouring in from
the ceiling and swirling all around the room. Hold the image of violet
Light until you see or feel or know the color white, gold, or pink. Go
further until the round walls of the room are entirely gone and you
have become the white, gold, or pink Light of Divine Love. Say, "I Am
free. I Am God, fully human, and I Am human, fully God."

THE PHYSICAL BODY

The physical body is the absorbent sponge for fear from the mental
body. The physical body absorbs repressed emotion, and together mental fear and emotional repression create imbalance, pain, and illness in
the physical body. The physical is usually the last body to heal from the
effects of fear. Angels have physical bodies made of Light and music. It
is our desire to help you remember how to transform yourselves so your
energy can flow and set you free. Athletes understand how to move
their **life force** freely in their bones and flesh so that they become more
flexible, faster, and more graceful. Imagine yourself as an athlete breathing in the Holy Spirit so emotion is free to unlock your vessel from fear.
Imagine your athlete self thinking, "Love is who I Am."

With a little practice, any human can be as free as an Angel. Perhaps
you were born with a physical body that remains stiff and slow to move.
When you use your imagination and your emotion to see, feel, and believe
that your physical body is free, you help us free all humankind. Humans
often feel their physical body holds them in like a prison. We are asked,
"How can my divine essence fit into this one small physical container?"
We are telling you how to stretch and how to open your physical body so
God's Light and Sound can help you to fly by expanding what appears to
be compact and dense. Your physical body is the sacred temple of God,
and the temple needs to be cared for as you would care for the most
expensive, precious material possession you own.

Remembering that you have a physical body is not always easy for human beings. Often you are living in the future your mental body is picturing for you. We ask you to ask your own Guardian Angels and your own intuitive voice to simply remind you to notice the house you are living in, your body. When you remember your body, picture yourself moving and allow space in your day for moving. It is not so important how you move, whether you dance, walk, jog, or swim. All that matters is for you to help the energy generated by your chakras to move. We recommend you do this with thought, feeling, and action. The human being is a spiritual vessel containing God's energy in thought (the mental body), in emotion (the emotional body), and in movement and form (the physical body).

 Expanding the Sacred Temple of God

See your physical body stretching very long and very wide. Breathe in deeply, and exhale slowly. Imagine yourself stretching all the body parts you can think of; it is like you are looking in different circus mirrors, stretching and breathing. Now see yourself dancing and flying freely in an open space filled with emerald green Light and coral Light. You can climb a mountain and swim across the sea, and you can run faster than an antelope, and you can move your body in any direction you delight in. Say, "I Am Divine, fully human. I Am human, fully Divine."

THE KEYS TO CREATING ONENESS WITHIN THE HUMAN VESSEL

Transformation and integration together make an incredible journey of evolution for the human self. We ask you to live courageously and stay focused on your process and progress moment by moment. When you do this, the mental body gradually lets go of time, and the human moves at Light speed on the path home to total freedom. Many teachers and healers are available to you, and we ask you to continue to seek the teacher and healer inside your higher self. The teacher is your intuitive channel connecting your spiritual body to your conscious thought. The healer is the unencumbered force of the Holy Spirit called your emotion.

The key to creating Oneness is to consciously will to transform each and every fearful thought in your entire mental body. As you transform the fear in your mental self—deep subconscious, subconscious, and conscious—you must will to clear fear from your emotional and physical bodies as well. Your own will is all you need to set you free. We do not promise you an easy path, yet we say it can be effortless if you allow it. Thought by thought, cell by cell, atom by atom, vibration by vibration, you must will to transform the fear hiding in your vessel by believing God is in charge.

Your very own OverSoul is directing your journey through the great schoolroom of Earth. When you ask your Angels to show you how every experience in your life is for your greatest good, you learn how to once again take responsibility back for your life and for your creation. As this happens, you begin to see your higher self as the master of your life, and all your heart desires begin to flow into your reality, the reality you are consciously creating.

We present you with the Angel Keys to human freedom. Can you achieve this freedom in this lifetime? It is entirely up to you and how willing you are to open. Please understand, God asks you to be willing, and willing does not mean you walk your journey alone. Willingness is an intention from your heart. At times, your mind will close again, but it will open when you choose to surrender. Surrendering to Mother Father God is allowing yourself to see the truth in what is happening to you. It is refusing to believe you are a victim of circumstance, and it is the development of great tolerance and patience for yourself for not learning as fast as your ego believes you should.

Freedom takes longer than the blink of an eye or snap of the fingers. Freedom requires you to heal the separation between you and your OverSoul, between you and God, layer by layer of misconception. We remind you that you have manifested into many atoms, cells, thoughts, feelings, and concepts about what is real. You must know. You must forgive. You must allow your whole vessel to be one with God and God's Universe.

We, the Twelve Archangels of the Central Soul, present you:

Our Angel Keys to Freedom of the Human Vessel

1. *Be willing and say often, "I Am surrendering to the will of God."*

2. *Be willing to take responsibility for every thought, feeling, and experience in your life,* both joyful and painful. We ask you to say often, "I Am surrendering to my highest joy and good."

3. *Demand to see the gift in all your experiences,* even the most tragic. Ask your intuitive channel, "What does this teach me?" "How does this help my heart to open?" "How is this for my greatest good?"

4. *Listen to your anger.* Your anger shows you where the Holy Spirit, the Divine force of emotion, is blocked inside you. We ask you to say often, "I Am releasing and I Am free."

5. *Remember time is an illusion that desires to trap you into fear again.* Masters and human beings never go backward on their path home to God. The journey takes just the right amount of time, and you are moving at just the right speed for your vessel.

6. *Ask for the miracle of balance between all the bodies in your vessel.* Be willing to ask for assistance in correcting imbalance wherever you discover it. We are always available, and when you need earthly help, we will help you find a healer who can assist in your rebalancing. We ask you to say, "I Am willing to experience the miracle of balance."

Book 5

Healing What Hurts

Learning How to Transform Your Karma

Often, Angels are accused of not understanding what it feels like to constantly face what you are most afraid of. In truth, we do understand. Suffering hurts, and longing brings more longing. We are here, walking with you, boosting your spirits, and whispering, "We love you and we know you can do it." You see, we too have touched humanity's deepest pain because we experience everything you do. This is the Law of One, and we are always and forever one with you. We know your fears, and we know how to show you the way home to complete and forever freedom. We know we can assist you in seeing Heaven before your eyes as well as inside everyone you meet.

Your Earth was originally designed as a schoolroom where Souls could come to experience separation from God. Souls now come to Earth to evolve beyond this illusion by transforming karmic debt. **Karma** means unfinished business; it is a summary of all lifetimes of all your thoughts, feelings, and actions where you believed fear was more powerful than God's love. Karmic debts are all the limitations—mental, emotional, and physical—you are experiencing during your life on Earth.

The human Soul is made of God's energy, God's Light and Sound. The law of karma requires your Soul to return to a place of Oneness with God. With each fearful experience, you leave a bit of your Sound and Light behind, and this law says you must bring all your Sound and Light back home to your human vessel, transforming all you know and all you believe about yourself.

Clearing your karmic debt requires you to integrate your ego and **shadow** with your heart center and free yourself from attaching to your limitations.

If you were born with physical birth defects, all that is asked of you is for you to go beyond these defects so they do not stand in the way of your service to humanity. When you do this, either the defects will completely disappear while you are on Earth, or your OverSoul will call you home to Heaven. When you return to Earth, you will have no physical defects. One day, human beings will have their full powers of physical body transformation restored. They will be able to repair their physical defects instantly, once the karmic debt is paid. This will be a joyful sign that Heaven and Earth are one.

Each incarnation, you return to Earth with a fresh start, an opportunity to completely finish all you need to finish. Each lifetime, we are responsible for pointing out to you parts of your Soul needing to come home. It is not necessary for you to remember your past lives. Your OverSoul designs any karmic lessons that you need to complete in this lifetime. If in a past life, for example, you sold your family into slavery, you will experience the emotional and mental and physical sensations of separation and abandonment. You will have an opportunity to forgive yourself and learn from the human perspective that separation and abandonment are illusions.

Many courageous Souls have returned to Earth, even though they have finished all their karmic lessons. These ancient ones have the memory and ability to move through karma, transforming it within themselves, for the purpose of raising mass consciousness. Yes, these Souls have already experienced Oneness on Earth, and still they have come back. They may or may not have the knowledge that their karma in this lifetime, their experiences of separation from God, is not of their own making. Karma is like lovely music being played with all the instruments out of tune.

The ancient ones joyfully returned to Earth to assist in tuning these instruments, although the lives they live are often full of challenge and change. How can human beings have compassion for the suffering of others if they, too, do not experience the ravage, the rape, the destruction, and the illusion of fear? As these Souls remember how to bring love into every thought, feeling, and action of their daily lives, the karma is transformed, and their Souls' vocation of helping humanity is successful.

We hope each of you will believe you are among these courageous Souls. Human beings have the potential to transform all the separation inside themselves and complete the service they have returned to do. Tuning instruments is a delicate job and requires a very good listening ear and sense of truth.

Karma is as karma does, and karma comes around quickly these days. You *will* be presented with the consequences of your choices, based on fear and made with ego, nearly instantaneously. Fear has put you to sleep and encouraged procrastination when dealing with your karmic lessons. No more! The Twelve Archangels and the faculty of schoolroom Earth demand that you do your own homework and do it now. Humanity is suffering greatly and the need to remember that you are God's children is imperative. Karma is merely illusion, an extraordinary set of screenplays written for you and by you to show you where you are still living in separation and denial of the God force. Transforming even the most diabolical and cruel lifetimes can be effortless when you are willing. Transformation requires love and service and setting your heart free.

Focus on this life, for this life is the key to all lives past and all lives forward. Tune your instruments for this life, and all the music you compose and play will be lovely and healing and perfect. This life is all you need to understand. Transform all the fearful experiences of this life—just the ones you remember will work quite nicely—and *you shall have no karmic debt,* no unfinished business to attend to.

We have one small exception to the above. As you become free, your heart will naturally yearn to assist others in their freedom. We call this "high karma," where your service to God facilitates the freeing of humanity and the creation of Oneness on Earth. We are delighted to come to the concert of all the instruments playing in tune, in perfect harmony with one another!

Will it be time for you to die and leave the Earth if all your work is done? We tell you, this is the time for play and celebration. Sit back, relax, and observe as Heaven and Earth fuse and are one again forever.

 Walking the Road of Forgiving Karma

Please take some slow, deep breaths and place both hands on your heart. Keep your hands on your heart. Imagine that a door opens to your left. When you stand at the doorway, you discover a large violet Flame appears next to you. As you move forward, the Flame moves with you. The path ahead looks rocky, with both hills and valleys to cross. Straight ahead, but in the far distance, is a cabin surrounded by trees of incredible beauty. As you walk towards the cabin, regrets of your past and fears of your present, will arise in your mind. Place each one into the violet Flame that is by your side. The Angel of Comfort and the Angel of Forgiveness will greet you when you arrive at their cabin. Make sure that the violet Flame stays by your side, breathe and trust.

FORGIVING THIS LIFETIME

Some experience Master Fear's allies of emotional and/or physical abandonment, neglect, and abuse at the moment of conception. Others may experience separation later in infancy, childhood, or adolescence. Why does separation from Mother Father God happen when the human is so young? The Soul enters the human being at conception, coming and going until the baby is ready to be born. Sometimes, the Soul changes its mind and decides to come at a later time. Whether this is by natural miscarriage, the mother's choice to stop her pregnancy, or by early death, **divine order** and God's will are still in charge.

The parents and the newly incarnated Soul have agreed to this experience, and we hope all concerned see the return of the new Soul as an opportunity for growth and forgiveness. Each birth of a human being happens because the OverSoul has decided to incarnate, to send God's Light and Sound to Earth to learn and facilitate Oneness.

Death and birth are never mistakes or accidents. The Soul always knows exactly what it needs to experience. To taste, touch, feel, smell, and know Master Fear is a gift the newly incarnated Soul agrees to give to humanity for the expansion and evolution of God. The reward for transforming fear back into love is allowing your vessel to experience forgiveness and love eternal.

Your Soul's heart is immune from fear. In your heart, you will find everlasting love in the face and the essence of the God Child within. God Child is a metaphor for the source of Divine Love and the key to forgiving all karmic debt for this life and all lives past and future. This **child within** your heart has your face and keeps all the memories of your life from time of conception and all knowledge of all experiences until your exit from Earth. Light and Sound are who this God Child is, and Light and Sound are what this child is here to bring to you. Abandonment, sorrow, unworthiness, and all other manifestations of separation from Mother Father God and God's Creation cover this Child of Divine Love in a dense, cloudy, and confused vibration. The covering is what many of your scholars refer to as the **inner child**.

We present you with how you can delicately, gently, and compassionately raise the vibration of separation belonging to the inner child to the glorious, joyful, and free vibration of the God Child.

First, we need you to acknowledge you have an inner child, an acknowledgment that you, too, have experienced feeling abandoned by God at some moment in your childhood or adolescence. We ask you not to compare your childhood with another's childhood. All are equal in the eyes of Mother Father God. Separation is an illusion. Abandonment is an illusion, as is physical, mental, and emotional suffering. This does not mean you did not truly suffer from tragic and trying experiences. It means illusion is not God's reality and therefore is easy to transform. You will experience and know and understand. As the process continues, all painful and embarrassing childhood memories will no longer have an emotional or mental distressing charge (effect) on your life. The memories will seem like old film footage that has no meaning to who you are and who you are becoming.

Second, we need you to practice the miracle of forgiveness and be willing to remember how to treat your human self as Mother Father God treats your Soul between each incarnation on Earth. Just as you have the God Child living within your heart center, you also have both a Divine Mother and Divine Father. Your Divine Mother and Father are aspects or faces of your own OverSoul and they, too, can be communicated with at will. As you embrace the child within, your heart opens the doorway between Earth and Heaven. Walk with us through this doorway, and your Mother and Father will greet you and take care of you. You are their only Child.

We hope you will participate in the Twelve Archangels of the Central Soul's reparenting class. Intend to heal completely and live on Earth as you do in Heaven. We will assist you in uncovering God's Child, and God's Child will introduce you to more of *you,* your Divine Mother and Father. One final step remains: meeting the Nature Angel who gives you life force or **chi** in physical manifestation. United once again, Mother God with Father God, one with Divine Love together with Creation; allow your human being to remember your own infinite worth. Knowing your family inside opens the door to connecting with all God's family living on your magic planet.

STARTING ALL OVER: REBIRTHING

What would your life be like if you could start it all over again, conceived in unconditional love, born into love, and raised in love? What would life feel like if you had never been exposed to fear's illusion of being separated from Mother Father God?

We begin by showing you how to gather your Soul's Sound and Light lost during conception, gestation, and birth. You are welcome to open your heart and will to do the imagery for your parents as well as for your siblings and children. We thank you for helping us rebirth humanity into total and complete unconditional love.

You are welcome to do this visualization again and again and fill your beginning with more Divine Love. Each time you use your will and intention to reconnect with Divine Love at the beginning of this incarnation, we promise you will experience greater freedom and mobility in your daily life. Each time you melt away the misconception that fear can influence how you live, who you are, and what you believe, you erase the effects of fear's negativity from your genetic coding. As the genetic code changes, you once again have a cellular, unconscious trust that Mother Father God supports you totally. When the deep subconscious trusts, the subconscious and the conscious follow, love fills your thoughts, and loving-kindness becomes your natural behavior.

Rebirth

Close your eyes, breathe in gentle and deep relaxed breaths, and breathe out completely. Say, "I Am one with Mother Father God."

Allow your hands to become God's hands, and breathe.

Open your hands, and allow the chakras in the center of your palms to relax. They will open and begin to pulse with Divine Love. Slide your fingers together so that your hands form a basket.

Into your joined hands, we place two cells of Light and Sound, one female and one male.

Love these two cells, breathe, and say, "I Am one with Mother Father God." See these two cells connect together.

See the cells multiply, adding more cells and becoming brighter. See the Light and Sound in them grow. Keep loving these precious cells of God's energy. Into these multiplying cells a brilliant white gold Light comes, your human Soul. Breathe and feel your hands pulse with love.

The bundle of cells and Soul unite and become one body. Hold this life in your hands, united with the hands of God.

Feel the divine fetus grow in these hands, breathe, and love this fetus. The divine fetus feeds on Divine Love pulsing from your hands and develops into a perfect expression of God's Creation.

At the moment you feel your divine baby is ready to be born, take your hands holding God's infant, and birth your new self into your heart. Your heart, united fully with the heart of God, receives your divine infant with *joy.* Feel this new divine life fill you and remake you.

Place your hands on your heart, and say, "We are one with Mother Father God. I Am born anew in pure and total Divine Love."

Feel your Guardian Angels holding you, loving you, and healing you.

We are one.

FORGIVENESS:
TRANSFORMING THE PAST, LAYER BY LAYER

Inside every human being is an innocent child, the child who trusts that his or her Soul is really immortal and Mother Father God is true and loving.

Layer by layer of separation between you and Oneness with God and God's Creation has been deposited on your powerful Soul. The innocent child within your heart, the child you may not even remember, begins to become lost in the fight to find a place in life on Earth.

Gradually, the outer chaos of the visible and tangible world takes over, and life becomes one reaction after another.

When your Soul chose your Earth family, you agreed to wear their layers of separation as well as those created from your own experiences. Whether this is your biological family or adoptive family, you agreed to believe in many of the family's concepts about how the world operates and how you are expected to function in this world. Before you were even born, you accepted your family's programming of caretaking of your physical, mental, and emotional bodies and you agreed to transform all neglect, denial, and fear contributing to this programming.

Life, since the moment of your birth, has been showing you what you believe about yourself and how you need to change these limitations and set your Soul free again. As you do this for yourself, you set your family of origin free as well.

The process of transformation is complete when you are no longer living in your past or attached and reacting to any experience in your present.

We invite you to look at all situations you find yourself reacting to and ask the question, "Does this feel familiar to me? Have I been here before?" We ask you to go back to your childhood, as far back as you can go and in as deep as your psyche will allow. Far and deep, and here is where you release, transform, and forgive.

Subconscious memories, memories from your past will surface up to your conscious awareness, and here you can visualize the colors of your chakras and work with Angel energy to set the child in your heart free. As the subconscious clears, the very deep subconscious cellular memories rise to the subconscious and may begin to show up in your dreams. With continued gentleness and patience, these cellular memories will surface to your conscious awareness, so again you can visualize the colors of your chakras and work with our power to clear away each layer of separation between you and God.

We ask you to say often, "I Am one with God."

We offer both a visualization for those who enjoy their imagination and a physical/emotional exercise for those who prefer working with feeling and for whom imagery is difficult. For working with Angel power, inner vision is not required, just intention to heal and free your vessel from fear. Know you are working with God's energy in the way that is for your greatest good!

Freeing God's Child

Take a deep breath in and exhale slowly. Repeat until you are peaceful. Close your eyes, and imagine you enter your heart chakra. This sanctuary is emerald green and open. Say, "I Am opening." Look in this sacred space for your little child. Is your child hiding and bruised? Is your child ready to embrace you?

With all your will, send love to your child and ask for forgiveness. Shower your child with violet Fire raindrops to begin to wash away the separation between you.

Ask this child to bring you all the hurting faces from your entire past, including past incarnations and hurting adult faces from this life. Bring these faces of you home into your heart. Shower each one with violet Light and say, "We are one with God. I Am home again."

Allow God's Child to be the guide of your life, and begin by traveling to your past. With each scene that appears on your mental screen, throw a violet Fire fireball and say, "I Am releasing. I Am transforming. I Am forgiving." Imagine that you stand together under a healing waterfall in a rainbow of all the chakra colors.

Ask your Guardian Angels (yes, you have more than one Guardian Angel) to show you where you gave your power over to fear in this life. Reclaim your power from when you were a child, an adolescent, young adult, and adult. Feel the truth within: you *are* one with God.

Ask your child to show you where you learned to devalue your human self, where you bought fear's illusion that humans are less than God. Say often, "I Am God, fully human. I Am human, fully God."

Know you are worthy of comfort, security, affection, abundance, and happiness. We thank you for remembering your worthiness and claiming what is yours.

As you transform your past, you transform your future, for you are the creator of your reality. Be brave, and transform the old programming on behalf of yourself and the human race. You deserve to live life on Earth as you do in Heaven.

The God Child is free when you remember with each thought, feeling, and physical movement to allow your heart to guide you and return you to a place of innocent trust.

Every painful experience is a miraculous gift to show you where the old programming is still inhibiting your freedom. Fight for your life! Remember, many brave Souls have returned to liberate humanity so all can live freely, so all can live in Oneness with God's Creation.

We invite you to try all exercises for connecting with your heart and healing the separation between you and God. We are hopeful you will find our exercises so delightful you will do them again and again and create new ones just for your beautiful child within your heart!

Outdoor exercise, nature setting, or music is recommended.

Dancing with Your Heart

If an outdoor sacred place is available to you, we invite you to go to that place, take off your shoes, and begin to walk in a circle.

Your circle has a starting point; walk your circle. Feel the ground beneath your feet as if you were doing this for the very first time.

Walk faster until you are dancing, moving your arms in all directions without purpose or agenda. Look at the scenery around you as if you were seeing it for the first time.

Sing to the child that is you.

 *Indoor Exercise*

Play your favorite music as loud as is comfortable for you. It is important for you to feel the vibration of the sound.

Lie down, stretch, and send love to any tight place or painful
place. Begin to rock your body, hug yourself, and then place your
hands on your heart. Rock as fast as you can and sound out any
sounds or words coming to you.

Breathe and stand up, stretch, and move.

Move as if you have just been released from a sarcophagus.

Stand under a warm, bright Light and imagine you are standing
in the sunshine. Feel the Sound and the warmth of the Light as if you
were doing this for the first time. Say, "I love you." Again and again.

INVITING IN THE DIVINE MALE
AND DIVINE FEMALE

To assist you in healing the separation between Heaven and Earth inside
your human vessel, we recommend you invite your Divine Mother and
Divine Father into your conscious awareness. These Divine Parents
teach you how to parent your human self with total, full-time, unconditional love and support.

The heart chakra is a doorway between Earth and Heaven. When
you walk through this door with your intention, you can connect with
the male and female energies of your OverSoul. As you open to the
energy of your Divine Male, the vibration of your thoughts begins to
shift from fear-based to love-based.

Connecting with your Divine Female will help you to unlock emotion in your vessel so that you can be nurtured with Holy Spirit and,
in turn, nurture your physical body, mental body, and emotional body.

Your OverSoul is your clearest spiritual guide for your return jou'
ney home. Ask to see (using your third eye chakra/inner vision) v

Divine Mother and Divine Father. They will communicate with you through intuitive thought and physical sensation. They can help you know when you are sabotaging yourself or neglecting the child within your heart. The more you open to your Divine Male and Divine Female, the faster you clear the old layers of fear's programming, and the easier your evolution on Earth becomes.

An important healing step to bringing in the all-loving, all-powerful and all-knowing energy of your Divine Male and Divine Female is to clear out negative old male and old female energy causing imbalance in your vessel.

Clearing out the Negative Old Male and Old Female Energy

Imagine you are looking in a mirror at the front of your body. The front and right sides of your vessel are male, and the back and left sides are female.

See your front morph into a great wardrobe filled with many drawers, shelves, and hanging clothes. All the spaces are filled with dusty, old male aspects that need to be transformed. In the drawers of your wardrobe you may see:

> More giving than receiving
> Needing to be better than others
> Inability to financially support yourself
> Fears about following your heart where career is
> concerned
> Old issues connected with your father
> Old issues connected to other male role models
> Lying to yourself or others
> Addictions—alcohol, drugs
> Shyness and fear of embarrassment
> Mental illness, obsessive worry, stress
> Unworthiness, low self-esteem

Trust your intuition to tell you what needs to be cleared away.

You have a fireman's hose hooked up to violet Fire, God's energy of transformation and forgiveness. Turn on the hose full-blast, and completely clear out the wardrobe until you see the emerald green Light of your heart chakra filling the wardrobe and pouring out into the room. Now, ask to meet your Divine Father and merge with his love and his power. Ask for his name, or give him a name, and together embrace and merge with God's Child, the child within your heart.

Now that you are united with your Divine Father and God's Child, see that you are now looking over your shoulder in the mirror. See the back side of yourself. Take your hose and with the violet Fire clear out the negative old female aspects of yourself.

Aspects of the old female may be:

> Repressed emotion
>
> Denial of feelings
>
> Difficulty in setting boundaries and
>
> > communicating boundaries
>
> Denial of physical beauty and sexuality
>
> Neediness
>
> Giving and receiving out of balance
>
> Denial of physical needs/self sacrifice
>
> Shortness of breath/exhaustion and physical
>
> > illness
>
> Shame
>
> Guilt
>
> Unworthiness
>
> **Victim-consciousness**
>
> Infancy and childhood issues with your
>
> > biological/adoptive mother and other female
> >
> > caretakers

Breathe in deeply, and exhale slowly; say, "I Am forgiveness."

Now, see God's Child, the child in your heart, handing you a ruby pink Light torch, and shine the Light into your clean wardrobe.

Watch the Holy Spirit completely redecorate your entire wardrobe, front and back. Step into the ruby pink Light and ask to meet your Divine Mother. Ask for her name, or give her a name. See yourself merge with her. Invite your Divine Male and God's Child to join in this union.

Say, "I Am one with Mother Father God, Divine Love and Creation. I Am the miracle of balance."

We hope you will clean out and organize your wardrobe often. Each time, you will clear more layers of separation between your human Soul and your OverSoul. Receive the Divine Love of your OverSoul into your vessel, and free your Divine Male and Divine Female so you can live freely. Free the innocent Child of God in your heart by transforming all the layers of fear you experienced in your past. Rebirth your infant, and begin a new life walking in love.

Rebirth, transform, and balance layer by layer.

Every painful or deceiving experience in your past carries a piece of your Soul's energy. Go find it and set humanity free! Your OverSoul presents you with a treasure hunt to discover all the riches and joy of the Kingdom of God's great Creation. You are this great Creation!

We walk beside you.

Book 6

The Human Soul

The human Soul begins every incarnation on Earth from the safe place of Heaven. On Earth, the Soul is asked to experience the cycle of birth and death before returning home. What humans often forget is that the Soul stays anchored in Heaven. And so the Soul has the opportunity and the power to merge Heaven and Earth together. We shall explain.

HEAVEN

Heaven is a very real place, a place filled with God's Sound and Light, a place where love is all that exists. Heaven is a vibration, a frequency of Sound and Light much higher than the vibration of Earth. In your human reality there exists both Heaven (Divine Love) and Earth. Fear causes the vibration of God's Creation to lower, to feel heavier and more solid, and this is why it appears that Heaven and Earth exist in two different places. We wish to help you understand that Heaven is real. It is possible for you to visit this place called Heaven, and it is possible for you to live in Heaven before you die.

As humanity surrenders fear and negativity to God's transforming love, humanity's vibration goes up, humanity becomes immune to fear's persuasion, and humanity experiences Divine Love everywhere. Humanity begins to live in Heaven.

Surrendering to the calling of your own Soul can assist us in our work to set you free.

Your Soul is connected to each and every Soul in the entire human race, just as each cell in your physical body is connected to all other cells. When cells in your physical body transform into malignant cancer cells, they stop listening to the cells around them. Some of these cells may isolate and form a tumor. Human Souls are very much like human cells.

The Soul in your human vessel is connected through an umbilical cord of Light and Sound to your OverSoul. The OverSoul is the source of God's energy that created your human Soul. Your OverSoul is your Soul's mother and father. Your OverSoul has the ability to restore your Soul, by teaching how to make wiser choices to your mind, and how to bring healing to every cell in your physical body.

When you use your human mind to activate the connection between your OverSoul and Soul, you will bring more Divine Love into your Soul each and every moment. Your OverSoul delights in nurturing you. Because your Soul touches all other human Souls, as your Soul is fed, it becomes easier for all Souls to activate their connection with their OverSouls. Eventually, all suffering of human Souls and cancer of human cells will be history.

We are asking for your assistance in accelerating this tremendous healing process!

Uniting of Souls

Please breathe in deeply and exhale slowly. Focus your mind on seeing a soft white gold Light. The Light is pouring out of a bowl, spilling over the sides and rising up as a fountain in the middle. Place a new bowl of Light to the South of this bowl, then one to the West, then North. Place the last bowl of Light to the East. Say, "Show me how Souls move. Show me how Souls connect here on Earth and in Heaven." Watch and enjoy!

EARTH

When your OverSoul decides to incarnate on Earth, two sacred energies are released from Heaven: the energy creating your Soul and the energy creating the Nature Angel or chi (life force) needed to manifest your physical body. The Nature Angel knows exactly what genetic coding you need to match your biological family. Your Nature Angel designs your physical temple with perfect accuracy, incorporating all mutations, limitations, and vulnerabilities you need to experience for your spiritual, emotional, and mental evolution during your life on Earth.

Encoded inside the cells of your physical body is a complete library of information of Mother Father God's experiment of duality on Earth. All you need to remember about the illusion of fear, as well as how to end separation in your earthly reality, is held within the cells of your body. Inside each cell is a map pointing out exactly where your Soul needs to go and what your Soul is here to accomplish. The map is always changing as you grow in consciousness and transform the fears you must face on the path home to God. As your Soul's map changes, you experience more moments of Heaven in your day. If you choose not to face your fears or if your ego gets caught too deeply in illusion, your Soul will make the choice for your life on Earth to end. This death will always happen as an emotional death first, giving your ego the chance to surrender and allow Divine Love into your human reality. Your human life will be rich with such opportunities to die and be rebirthed at a new level of consciousness, more awake and closer to your divine self. If you cannot surrender (an example is being addicted to drugs), and your overall vibration is going down instead of up, your Soul and Nature Angel will leave your physical body, taking your consciousness back to Heaven where your education will continue.

Freedom is the ultimate goal of your Soul's evolution of discovery. It is always a great gift when you make the choice to evolve and grow with your Soul.

Your OverSoul, together with your Guides, teachers, and loved ones in Heaven, and Guardian Angels (Angels that protect you in each incarnation) plan your earthly journey in great and perfect detail. All experiences are designed to help you remember where you come from and where you are going. Your OverSoul makes contracts and agreements for all the Souls you will connect with. These contracts are to work synergistically to facilitate the remembering for both of you. Their plans allow for no mistakes, as they are created in Heaven. You will make no mistakes in your life. You will have no accidents, for your OverSoul is always guiding you through fear back to eternal love.

LIFETIME

Your journey is not bound by the limitations of one lifetime. Your Soul will return as many times as needed to achieve freedom from fear. We are hopeful you will live this life as if it were your last. We see your Soul achieving freedom this life!

More than one visit to Earth has been necessary for you to fully experience how Master Fear tries to control the consciousness of humanity. More than one visit to Earth has been required for you to remember that love always wins over evil. Each human Soul has access to the lives of all other incarnations, so even if you believe this visit is your first, your Soul remembers millions. All Souls will achieve freedom, and it will feel as if it happens at the same time, during the same life, for all people. We believe the time has come!

DEATH

From our perspective, humans are dead until they free their minds and bodies of fear. Each time you choose to believe fear has power over you,

you are committing suicide. Every moment you choose love and trust in God's plan, you become more alive. We see you resurrecting yourself from death. We see humanity rising up from the grave of fear and dancing the celebration of life on Earth.

Physical death is another mystery. First, we need you to understand what being physical is all about.

Inside your Soul chakra, located in the navel area of your abdomen, live your human Soul and your Nature Angel. Your Nature Angel is responsible for expressing God's Sound and Light by giving you a form called your physical body. Nature Angels use **creation energy**, also called the chi or life force, to give you a vessel on Earth and in Heaven. To hold God's energy in the form of matter, your Nature Angel lowers the vibration of energy to what humans perceive as solid and tangible. Death comes when your physical body has absorbed or experienced all the fear it can hold, and your chi burns out, just like a candle.

The OverSoul calls the human Soul back to itself, and your Nature Angel returns to Heaven to create a new body for you. Because this new body exists at Heaven's high vibration of pure love, it appears you have left the Earth entirely. Your old physical body remains at the vibration of Earth and is recycled back into basic components of physical matter. When your Soul returns to Heaven, all of your loving thoughts and feelings of Oneness with other human Souls, and the Earth herself, travel with you.

Likewise, all your fearful thoughts and any blocked emotions remain on the Earth. Because your Soul is responsible for your whole human vessel, you are given the opportunity to work with your Angels and Guides to clean up any negativity you left behind on the Earth.

We call this your "Soul gathering." We hope you will choose to gather all the abandoned thought, emotion, and creation/action energy of your human Soul while you are still living on Earth. Again, as you take responsibility for your vessel, you assist all humanity in raising the vibration of Earth to that of Heaven. Heaven is coming closer every day.

As you intend to gather your Soul's Light and Sound by transforming the fear in your human vessel, your conscious mind fuses with your higher mind, the mind of your OverSoul. As you allow more love to flow into your vessel, your human Soul opens to receiving more and more Sound and Light from your OverSoul. When the OverSoul and human Soul unite as one on Earth, it is possible for the chi to burn forever. What is more important than immortality on Earth is the choice to live a heavenly life while you are here.

You are already immortal. Your Nature Angel has the ability to create a physical body at will, anywhere you need to exist in the Universe. You can also decide to merge the physical body/creation energy, mental body/thought energy, and emotional body/Holy Spirit energy back into your spiritual body and again exist as Divine Love, the pure energy of God's Sound and Light. The challenge here is that doing this is not your ego's choice to make. This is all about Soul, where your Soul needs you to be at any given moment or at any dimension of reality. Trust us, many human Souls are living more than one life at a given time and space on your planet. Focus on where you are now and what your Soul is asking you to learn from the experience that you are living. If you need to learn about another life or experiences in a different time and space, your higher self will show you in dreams or in meditation. All experiences are designed by your OverSoul for you to learn, evolve, and grow in consciousness.

Fear creates the illusion of separation between your Soul and the OverSoul. Fear causes your vessel to die, and love allows you to live. Be brave enough to know your Soul and walk together consciously on your path home to Heaven. Heaven is life, and we believe now is the moment for humanity to truly live!

Doing the following exercise will *not* speed up your physical death. This exercise will help your ego receive death gracefully when your Soul has decided that your lessons for this incarnation are over.

❁ Graceful Death

Please breathe in deeply and exhale all fear of death. See Heaven's doorway open. Your Divine Male, Divine Female, and Divine Child are standing in the doorway. Look down at your feet and take off your shoes. Put on the ruby Light slippers waiting for you. Dance through the doorway into the gold white Light of Divine Love. Go to them and rejoice!

BEING ALIVE

Being truly alive is exactly what you are ascending into. Angels define **ascension** as freedom on Earth. Many human Souls have achieved freedom from fear and have evolved into Heaven's vibration. They walk with you on your Earth, touching you, and sending you messages, "Heaven and Earth are one."

They say to you, "Trust in Mother Father God and see the reality of total love." As you continue to take responsibility for transforming your fearful thoughts and reactions into loving thoughts and faith, these ascended Souls become part of your conscious reality. An ascended human Soul has become a master over fear and is immune from fear's trickery.

Every human Soul is an ascending master. We remind you often, masters never go backward on their path home. Thank you for helping us to help the graduating class of humanity ascend out of Earth's schoolroom of separation into Earth's playground of love everlasting!

The Twelve Archangels of the Central Soul invite you to attend our class on Soul gathering.

An Angelic Course for Ascending Masters
REQUIREMENTS

1. Determination to free your human vessel from fear's illusions
2. Courage to follow God's will, the will of your heart
3. Willingness to take responsibility for creating your outer reality
4. Willingness to transform all negative and fearful thoughts into love and Oneness

5. Willingness to unlock Holy Spirit and free your emotional body

6. Willingness to learn how to nurture your physical temple and treat your body with love and respect

7. Willingness to trust that God lives in everyone and that all people have equal potential for successfully completing this course

8. Accepting and trusting that all human Souls are automatically enrolled in our course for ascending masters (awareness of what humanity is doing on Earth helps humanity graduate at Godspeed)

CLEARING UNWORTHINESS FROM THE SOUL CHAKRA

Unworthiness is a belief—deep subconscious, subconscious, and sometimes conscious—that the value of being human is less than being an Angel, less than Mother Father God. With this belief, the human Soul remains separate from God, God's Creation, and the divine destiny for the human self.

Held within your Soul is tremendous knowledge describing the details of how you are called to break free of fear and fear's illusions. The Soul understands it must assist the mental body in clearing away fear's concepts of unworthiness, defeat, inequality, and separation. The Soul actively creates with the OverSoul outer- and inner-life challenges to accomplish freedom on all levels.

The Soul chakra supplies Divine Love to both your Soul and chi force. Together, the Soul and chi give your entire vessel creative, sexual, and life-nurturing forces. These combined forces are called the kundalini. When the Soul chakra is blocked by low vibration energy produced from fearful thought, the **kundalini energy** can short-circuit.

When the kundalini forces are disturbed, the mental body has great difficulty in transforming fearful, negative, and victim-consciousness thinking. The creative flow of ideas coming through from the higher mind of the OverSoul is continuously interrupted. When this flow is interrupted, it is difficult for the mind to stay focused and identify what actions are needed to manifest the creative ideas.

The emotional body becomes blocked, and the Holy Spirit cannot flow throughout the entire vessel. This can create feelings (messages to the mental body) of depression, hatred of self and others, deep despair and loneliness and intense isolation from other human beings or nature or both.

If the kundalini energies are short-circuiting in the physical body, the physical body may be attracted to chemical substances, pain, and abusive sexual relations. Blocked kundalini can contribute to slothfulness of the physical self as well as illness.

Disruption of the kundalini flow can contribute to addiction to substances, activities, thought patterns, and relationships to animals, people, and material possessions. One such addiction is that of self-sacrifice and the reverse, unbalanced receiving or greed.

About human sexual relationship, we ask you to remember that when two people are sexual, they are sharing their kundalini energy. Kundalini is a most powerful and sacred manifestation of Divine Love. We encourage you to know and love your whole vessel before you share your Soul in sexual exchange with another. It is not enough to love with the mind. Love with your whole vessel, and both partners will benefit greatly from the synergistic sharing of Soul and chi!

 Transforming and Freeing the Kundalini Energy

Lie down, close your eyes, and breathe. Fill your mind with violet Fire and say softly, "I Am love."

Invite your Divine Male and Divine Female to open the Soul chakra.

Empty all that binds your Soul with your intention, "I Am love."

Become one with every gram of unworthiness in your entire vessel.

Say, "Unworthiness, come forth into the Light and Sound of God."

Can you feel the darkness that chokes the sacred kundalini? Release the darkness by breathing in violet Light deep down into your belly. Do this with all the power inside you. See yourself filled and surrounded with blazing violet Fire. And next see your entire body filled and surrounded with ruby red Holy Spirit. And now the white gold Light of Divine Love.

Say, "I Am completely one with Divine Love."

Imagine you are bathing in a beautiful coral, peach Light, the Light of Peace and Serenity. This is the kundalini Fire. Let it flow up and down your vessel, out through the soles of your feet, the palms of your hands, and the crown of your head. See it pouring out of and into each cell of your body, cleansing fear away from your body and life.

You may drift off to sleep for a short time while your OverSoul adjusts your vibration. When you feel complete and ready to rise, say softly, "I Am love."

MEETING YOUR NATURE ANGEL AND STRENGTHENING THE CHI

Each human vessel provides a home for a Nature Angel, and this Angel gives creation energy to the human being and provides you with a vessel, or physical body. We remind you, a human is God's energy in four aspects: Divine Thought, Divine Emotion, Divine Love, and Creation. Creation energy unifies thought, emotion, and love and generates physical matter, such as stars, planets, human beings, animals, plants, and rocks.

The Nature Angel governs the chi or life force energy for your physical body. When you respect your body as God's great Creation, your Nature Angel allows the flow of the chi to increase. Your body needs to move, dance, exercise, and be touched by human beings. Asking your Nature Angel to teach you Creation's way of nurturing your body helps the life force to flow and makes moving, dancing, and exercising effortless. Your Nature Angel is willing to help you be a true disciple of treating your physical body as a precious temple containing God's Divine Love.

Inside you lives God's Child, and the child must play and receive physical affection. You can do this by massaging your own body and welcoming affection from people and Angels you trust. We present you with how your Nature Angel can help you take better care of your physical temple and bring you eternal youth. As you nurture and exercise the muscles of God's house, you help clear the Soul chakra of unclear and blocked kundalini energy. God's Child knows your Nature Angel, and God's Child understands the Soul. Allow this child to play, and increase the flow of the chi so the sacred kundalini can keep you human, fully God, and God, fully human.

 ### Communicating with Your Nature Angel

Close your eyes, breathe air deep into your abdomen, and exhale completely. Continue to breathe and focus on your breathing.

Place your hands on your Soul chakra, just below the navel, and imagine finding a door underneath your hands. Ask the child of your heart for the key to open this magic door. Take the key and see yourself and God's Child walk through the sacred door. Say, "I Am here to meet my life force." Send love to your Nature Angel, and allow the love to grow and flow back to you. Say, "I Am life force, free and immortal."

It is not important whether you actually see your Nature Angel. Trust that you will feel the chi energy in time, or see this Angel, or both.

Ask your Angel to assist you in taking excellent care of your physical body. Remember to ask for your Angel's name so you can call on him or her to help you exercise effortlessly and stay disciplined. Ask that all the food you eat be filled with health and love. Ask your Angel to let any food your body doesn't need to pass on through so that you metabolize only what is for your vessel's greatest good and highest joy. Listen for guidance from your Nature Angel on any health concerns you have.

Your Nature Angel is your own personal trainer, nutritionist, and whole-body healer, all in one. Many healers of the physical body are available to you, and we are hopeful you will remember to check in with your own internal expert to ensure you are receiving the best type of assistance for *your* body.

ONENESS

As your OverSoul fuses with your Soul and your Soul assists your physical, mental, and emotional bodies to resurrect from death, all the Earth rejoices. Because of your faith and courage, you help all people to live free of fear.

As your OverSoul fuses with your Soul and your Soul and Nature Angel send forth the sacred kundalini, all the Earth celebrates. Because of your discipline and love, you help all people create a new human body. This human body is free of disease, free of cancer, and free of death.

As your OverSoul fuses with your Soul and your Soul connects with God's Child in your heart, God in four aspects is completely unified within your human vessel. Because of your will to transform your thoughts into Divine Thought, your feelings into Divine Emotion, your action into Divine Love, and your physical body into God's temple, you bring Heaven and Earth together.

As your OverSoul fuses with your Soul, you consciously begin to connect with all people and all Mother Father God's Creation. Because of the Oneness inside of you, you create Oneness and all the blessings of Heaven in all your experiences. You experience love with every breath; in every moment, you live in joy.

Welcome to Heaven!

It is the will of God for humanity to remember God is a most magnificent spiral of Sound and Light, a symphony playing joyful music, and your Soul is a most critical instrument in the orchestra!

ANGEL MESSAGES

Divine Intervention in Daily Life

Practical Application of the
48 Angel Messages

The 48 Angel Messages are designed to be a quick reference guide for accessing Angelic guidance where needed. Like the Treasury, the writing of the messages was inspired by my twenty-five years of private practice together with my passion for teaching with the Angels. The special feature of the messages is that we can ask the wounded child (subconscious mind) to show us exactly where we are blocked and how to transform the block by opening to a random message. It is my experience that our higher self and Guardian Angels make sure we choose the correct message. Working with the messages in this way offers a practical and invaluable method for helping the self move out of the past and into abundance.

It was the mission of the Angels and myself to offer guidance that really supports everyday life. Angels do understand what it means to be human. The assistance provided in the 48 Angel Messages is practical and very effective at shifting our vibration closer to the goal of unconditional love for self, others, Mother Earth, and the Universe.

❖❖❖

Message 1

THE HOLY SPIRIT

*T*oday we remind you to breathe, to breathe in deeply and exhale slowly. Angels live forever because their food is Holy Breath, love, and music. We offer this nourishment to you in great abundance. Feast on Holy Breath by remembering to breathe as Angels do, deeply filling ourselves with Holy Spirit, divine essence of Mother God. The air you breathe, no matter how polluted your scientists report it to be, is filled with Holy Spirit. Mother God's energy stays fresh and pure because this is her way of feeding her sweet children of Earth.

Magic happens when you remember with each breath you inhale, you are bringing in Mother God's love into every atom, thought, feeling, and sense of yourself. Awareness of what you are really doing when you breathe will make a profound difference in your life. When you are aware of Holy Spirit, fear melts away, as does disharmony, disease, and depression. We wish to add that if you discover you are forgetting to breathe, fear has entered or surfaced from somewhere inside your mind. Whisper the word "Angel," or the word "God," and we will come and remind you to breathe in deeply and exhale slowly, breathing as a happy, free Child of God.

We love you and wish you a joyous day.

 Divine Mother Love

Close your eyes, and begin to breathe slowly and deeply. See yourself resting on a ruby pink cloud of Light. Invite Mother God to love you, to hold you, rock you, and feed you from her heart. Visualize her pink Light of purest love saturating your entire being inside, outside, and all around you. Whisper the words "I love you" to the little child who lives within your heart. He or she is the child of the Divine Mother.

Message 2

CREATIVITY

*E*ach individual Soul expresses the creative force of God in a unique manner. When the creative door of the Soul is opened, God's voice begins to flow from your very own divine music box. When you listen to this magnificent music, life can become a miraculous manifestation of the highest ideals of your mind and purest desires of your heart. The music of the Soul is a metaphor for your creative potential. Holding the intention of sharing this music with others will awaken hidden talents of great value.

This new discovery of higher self is likely to invite fear's voice of doubt to cause the lid of Soul's music box to catch on its hinges. Fear confuses the ears so you may question, "Is this truly God's voice I hear? Are these truly my talents to share with humanity?" We wish to help you open your music box of creativity by clearing the fear away.

Angels are here to show you how to ignite the creative force of your Soul and let your unique music play for all the world to hear. It is your birthright to be prosperous, filled with purpose, and living your greatest potential. Join us, and free God's song of everlasting creativity.

Creative Expression of God

Begin to breathe in a lovely golden Light. Bring the Light all the way to your toes, and when you exhale, see the gold Light gently swirl all around you. Say, "I Am opening." See the gold Light sparkle like flakes of gold in the sun. Allow yourself to dissolve into sparkles. Take a great deep breath and see yourself come back into your body. See yourself expanded, new and full of fiery coral Light. Proclaim, "Yes, I Am the creative expression of God!"

❖❖❖

Message 3

SURRENDER

*D*uring times of stress, humans ask us if God has any understanding for humanity's misery and desperation. Through your life lessons and human suffering, you are challenged to discover the indestructible God fiber within you. Your greatest moments of hopelessness are also your deepest moments of surrender. Surrender brings you awareness and insight into your truth, and it is through total surrender to Mother Father God within you and all around you that the greatest miracles happen.

Earth is a schoolroom where you are asked to evolve in consciousness. This process of evolution needs you to stretch and grow out of your comfort zone. We ask you to take big leaps of faith, face the unknown, and let go of needing to know how to get where your ego wants to go. Choosing to surrender the wants of your ego to the true desires of your heart will help you to see that God knows best for you. Welcoming the changes that are for your greatest good is part of learning to surrender. The joy of surrendering to *change for the better* will see you through any dark night.

Total surrender is about taking a deep breath and stopping the mind, letting go of control, and believing in the mercy and divine wisdom of your God self. In these moments where you are willing to give up everything you believe you know, we see you expand the most. Expansion of your faith will set you free from physical, emotional, and mental prisons so that you are ready to believe life is worth living again.

Yes, we promise to assist you, dear Child of God! We present you with a recipe for surrender. The Angelic Kingdoms responsible for the healing of Earth, together with Master Buddha co-created a magical resting spot for suffering humans to voice their frustrations to Mother Father God. Buddha and the Angels call this sacred place the "garden of compassion." The garden is accessible through your desire and imagination. All who are sad and feeling hopeless are welcome to come and profess their hurts to Beings of Light.

 ## *Garden of Compassion*

Breathe in slowly and exhale deeply. Focus on your breathing until you feel calm and centered. Lie down on a huge emerald stone. Close your eyes and say, "I Am surrender." Golden Angels come and carry you to the garden of compassion. The Angels of the garden welcome you to bare your heart and tell us your troubles. Breathe in the healing Light, and exhale the discontentment. Open to the golden Light, and see it fill your heart, mind, and body. Say, "I invite miracles to come to me in abundance. I welcome the peaceful feeling of sweet surrender."

Message 4
TRANSFORMATION

*H*umans have been conditioned to believe that seeing is believing. What you can see, feel, touch, taste, and hear constitutes what is reality because you perceive your outer world as finite, solid, and slow to change. Human reality is more like a movie, an illusionary documentary filled with passionate drama. The dramas in your life's movie are seductive and consuming, and sometimes we see you believing drama is all there is. Angels and Guides and other assorted Beings of Light hope to help you untangle yourselves from the great spiderwebs of human drama by reminding you to edit your documentary anytime you choose.

Life's movie feels like permanent reality when humanity forgets Earth is a schoolroom designed to teach you where you are still separate from your heart, your will, and your confidence. It is our deepest desire to show you that, as children of God, you always have choice—no matter how unchangeable life's situations seem to be. A whole new world of experiences awaits you each time you challenge your fears and break through the illusion of your attachments.

Often, your past experiences flavor your aspirations for tomorrow. We will teach you how to transform these past experiences so you need not carry them into your future. We will show you how to transform your fears into love, and quickly your drama will become a comedy of illusions. Come and allow us to show you the way out of the wilderness of your attachments, broken dreams, and impossibility. Let us walk with you into your new reality of conscious choice and conscious freedom. Make a new movie with scenes overflowing with hope, joy, and richest experience.

 Walk in the Purple Forest

Breathe in slowly and exhale completely. Close your eyes, and see yourself walk into a beautiful green forest. The branches of the trees knit together over your head, creating a magical tunnel. Walk under the trees, and see the groon change to a brilliant violet. The violet Light is the Angel power of transformation and forgiveness. As you walk under the violet canopy, imagine a gentle violet-colored rain of Light beginning to fall from far above you. Walk in the gentle rain, breathing in the transformation and forgiveness, and know this energy of God is transforming your fears, regrets over your past, and anxieties concerning your future. Love will set you free and put you on a new path to everlasting joy.

Stay in the violet Light as long as you like, walking in the purple forest with the rain washing all the drama away. Say, "I Am *free!*" Angel energy is magical and miraculous, and so we invite you to visit this experience often. The more frequently you partake of Heaven, the faster you see results in your daily life.

Message 5

COMING HOME

*O*n the days that the analytical mind demands control, the ego self releases with full force the judging, comparing, and wanting torpedoes. These torpedoes are thoughts that explode in your head, demanding that you must know what is going to happen next. Before you take your next breath, your thoughts are racing down Scenario Lane, searching for the right house where you can hide safely and prepare yourself for all the worst that can happen.

The ego is the part of your mind that identifies itself as separate from God and Creation. It holds within it your personality and how you see yourself in your outer world. The ego mind has great potential for leading you away from your center, that intuitive all-knowing space where you feel kindred with the Universe.

When you are thinking from your center, your head and heart are connected to your inner voice. This voice of God within you has all the answers to all the questions, and when you obey this voice, you are always living your life for your highest joy and good. When you live life from your center, a calm, peaceful, and confident feeling radiates out from your whole self. In this place, you are home and focused on the moment. The center has no room for fear because you are moving with the flow of God, and everything is in place for you.

In truth, your ego was designed to find its way home to God. We desire to show you how to integrate your ego self, your beautiful, questioning human personality, with your center, the home of God within you. As the ego and center become united again, you will discover the tremendous power of staying present and in tune with all of the Universe.

To open and expand the Center of God within you, the umbilical cord of Christ-Buddha Light of Divine Love must be connected from your heart to the heart of Mother Father God.

Bringing Ego Home

Please breathe in deeply and exhale slowly. See yourself standing under a brilliant white golden Light. See yourself stretching up to greet the Light, and allow the Light of Divine Love to flow into your head and travel all the way down into your feet. The white golden Light is now pouring in, completely filling you until it overflows out through every pore of your body. It even flows out through the soles of your feet and palms of your hands.

Gently, with deep slow breaths, allow yourself to totally dissolve in the love. Say, "I Am home, ego come home with me," again and again until you feel relaxed, clear, and peaceful all over.

Message 6

DIVINE ORDER

*E*very event in the Universe, seen and unseen, is perfectly orchestrated by the will of Mother Father God. Divine will, or divine order, is the highest form of government for humanity, and no earthly laws can negate Mother Father God's will. When you consciously choose to obey God's will by listening to the voice of God within you, you will know and trust that each and every experience in your life happens for the greatest good of all concerned.

Often, it is difficult for humans to know their truth, and yet all that is needed is a sincere intention to listen to your God self. Divine order will miraculously choreograph life's lessons until you see, feel, know, and trust your truth and understand how to live your divine will right here on Earth.

Mother Father God, within you and all around you, supports every moment of your life with unconditional love. Every Child of God has a divine destiny, a purpose for being here. As you learn to have faith again in divine order, you break free from believing you are a victim of circumstance or a victim of your past. It is God's will for you to live life free from fear and fear's entrapment of separation from Oneness.

Ask to know God's will in the decisions you make in your daily life, and ask to understand the divine order in your past experiences. Your path home to living in Heaven here on Earth will be Lighted with truth, and you will know what actions to carry out for the greatest good of all.

Sapphire Ocean

We introduce you to Archangel Michael, Angel of the Lord. The word "Lord" means "the will of God." Michael's energy protects the truth and establishes God's law and order here on Earth. Begin by closing your eyes, taking some slow deep breaths, and placing your right hand on your heart, with your fingers touching your throat. Archangel Michael places his hand on your hand. See his lovely sapphire blue color, God's Light of will and truth, flowing out from the palm of your right hand into your throat and into your heart. Know Michael's Fire is burning through any obstacles to truth in your mental, emotional, physical, and spiritual body. As Michael fills you with will, see the Light become a great sapphire blue ocean, and you are a dolphin swimming in divine purpose, destiny, freedom, and truth.

As you swim in the great ocean, say, "I Am the will of God" over and over and know that your higher will blazes out as a great blue Flame of truth for all the world to see.

Message 7

LISTENING
TO YOUR INTUITION

*Y*our all-knowing intuitive truth lives deep inside your creative mind and speaks out to you constantly, no matter where you are or what you are doing. This well of guidance is available to you when you remember to listen, to listen without talking. Thoughts are very talkative, and often they compete for your attention. It can be quite challenging to distinguish between the soft and subtle intuition and the boisterous, nonstop chatter of conscious thoughts.

Conscious thoughts are like a committee of experts who give you a list of tasks you need to do and at the same time offer suggestions on how to avoid doing the tasks for a little longer. Listening to these experts may seem like listening to a room filled with supervisors ordering you here and there, pointing out what you are not doing fast enough or well enough.

In contrast, intuitive thoughts are gently whispering all the answers to all your questions and pointing you to your truth, the path of least resistance, the direction for the highest joy and good of all. Your intuition always knows the easy way of doing everything you need and want to do. Intuition allows your heart and mind to connect and your body to be calm and centered.

We are here to teach you how to experience these amazing thoughts of clear insight and total uncompromisable truth twenty-four hours a day. The practice begins with taking a steady and deep inhale and then exhaling completely. Focus your attention on listening by sweeping aside any thoughts traveling through your mind, an experience similar to tuning out the voice of a boring lecturer. Politely escort out any memories arising from the past or thoughts of the future. Allow your awareness to drift as if in a daydream into the blank space you have just created and ask a question. Any question will do, and one we recommend you ask is, "What is my purpose here on Earth?"

You may also wish to ask the question, "What do I need to do for the greatest benefit of all concerned today?" The intuitive voice is infinite, all-knowing, and perfect in its accuracy. The more you listen to your intuition, the louder and more discernible it becomes. Eventually, the experts of the conscious mind will be quiet and follow the directions given by the voice of God within you.

Engaging Intuition

Begin to breathe in deeply and exhale slowly. Focus all of your attention on your spinal column, all the way from your head down to your sacrum. Try to feel your whole spine at the same moment. See the brilliant white Light of Divine Love flowing into the top of your head and pouring down your spine, and feel your entire spine melt like a stick of butter in the warm sun. Keep breathing and melting and listen, just listen, and ask a question. Listen and breathe and melt and know.

❖❖❖

Message 8

HOW TO LOVE A
HUMAN BEING

*W*e have discovered how very little humans understand about loving humans. Human beings have three basic requirements for survival: affection, attention, and acknowledgment. Being a most miraculous invention of God, you are composed of love, and the more you remember how to love your whole self—your mental, emotional, physical, and spiritual bodies—the faster you create your happiest dreams-come-true.

In every adult human lives a Child of God wanting to experience the miracle of unconditional love. You can begin to learn how to love this child inside you by practicing unconditional loving on your family, friends, coworkers, enemies, and strangers.

Angelic Beings love only unconditionally, and so we present you with how we love you. First, Angels love humans by giving them all the space they need to learn their lessons. We have no expectations for your behavior because we understand you are behaving just as you need to. We do not judge you or question your judgments, nor do we compare you to any other human, for we know you are the only one like you. It is impossible for you to be just like anyone else, and as all Children of God are created from Divine Love, inequality simply does not exist. The most important thing about how Angels love is that we have no expectations for how or when or where you are supposed to love us back.

The great expectation your Divine Mother Father has for you is that you will choose to love yourself unconditionally, follow your heart's desires, and live on Earth as you do in Heaven.

When you love someone, the love will always come back to you, but not always in the way you expect. Humans spend a great deal of time trying to define the nature of their relationships, and we tell you all of your relationships are family relationships. Each human being wants to be loved and respected and feel important enough to you to receive your focused attention, affection, encouragement, and appreciation. Allow the love you give to each member of the human family to return to you in its own time and own way.

Surrender your expectations, open your heart, and *love one another.* Love given as a gift without strings attached will multiply and flow back to you in joyful abundance.

Playing in Pink Love

Breathe in deeply and exhale slowly. Close your eyes, and see yourself enter the door of your heart. Inside the door, you will find a little child wanting to receive your love and affection. Scoop this beautiful Being of Light up in your arms, and together walk to a pool filled with pink Light, the Light of unconditional love. Together, slip into the pool, and stand under a beautiful pink Light waterfall. Laugh and play in the pink energy. Soak up the Light until you both feel completely pink through and through. Enjoy the feeling of pure love, given and received so freely. True love is all there is. And *love, love, love* is all a human needs.

Message 9

IMAGINATION

*I*magination is the window through which seers, prophets, and clairvoyants receive visions from God. This window can work like a tunnel or doorway linking the human mind to the inner planes, the dimensions beyond what is here on Earth. Imagination creates images from thought; therefore, for a human being to receive accurate images untouched by fear and by the ego mind's control, it is always wise to ask to see only what is for the greatest good and highest truth for Oneness.

Angels believe that now is the time for all of humanity to remember how to send messages to God through images. When you link the creative force of the imagination with your intuition, God's voice within you, you open up a source of miraculous creative power.

We ask you to clear your mind of all negative thoughts and impressions. Think of a miraculous experience you wish to have happen for yourself or someone you love. Picture the experience with your imagination, and then send the image to us. The vision of the desired experience is then presented to your OverSoul, the part of you never separated from Oneness. Your miracle will manifest in the time and manner for your highest joy and good, and often you experience something even better than what you asked for.

Start each day with imagining, sending images to God, of all you would like to experience. See yourself living a brand new life in total freedom and joy here on Earth. Help us to help you create your heart's desires and make them come true!

We remind you of a basic truth: Your past is gone, and your future is not here yet. If you ask to see your future, be open to something even better. If you see visions of your future, understand we often speak to you in symbols. Keep looking through the window, and the window becomes the door. Understanding will come. Trust what you see, follow your heart, and know at all times that only your greatest good can come to you.

 ## Purple Hat of Truth

Close your eyes, and see yourself placing a bright violet hat on your head. The purple hat is an image that activates the violet Fire, God's energy of transformation, of your own crown chakra. This energy can work like a filter to eliminate all fearful thought so you can send and receive images of truth.

Breathe in slowly, exhale completely, and continue to picture the hat of violet Fire. When your mind feels free, imagine a beautiful place where you would love to take a vacation. See yourself resting in complete peace and serenity, and then ask your Angels to show you a vision concerning you, an insight you have been waiting for.

Message 10

GRATITUDE

*H*uman beings have the divine destiny to live on Earth in complete freedom and harmony. It is your birthright to have all the money, material resources, loving relationships, good health, and inspiring work your heart needs and wants.

The fastest way to jump over fear's obstacles of poverty of spirit, mind, and body is to practice gratitude. Gratitude is about giving thanks for everything you experience and taking the time to allow these experiences to show you where you are still buying into fear's illusions. Because your planet is a schoolroom, you can use the power of gratitude to learn what you need to learn from separation and move on to living a heavenly life right in your own living room.

Practicing gratitude brings a new perspective into dying and impossible situations. Giving thanks and trusting that each and every lesson is for your greatest good melts the resistance of the ego self and sends the shadow self running. The shadow self is the voice inside that tries to sabotage your faith in your higher self and in God.

The magical energy of gratitude will catapult you out of nearly every stagnant situation you find yourself trapped in. It is the secret to speeding up your evolution, and it is the key to ascension. Give thanks for all that delights you and all that annoys you and terrifies you as well, and you will ascend out of all the illusion that separates you from receiving your divine destiny, your birthright as a Child of God.

🌸 *Rainbow of Gratitude*

Breathe in slowly and deeply. Exhale fully and take another long and deep breath. Continue to focus on your breathing until you feel centered. To bring in the vibration of gratitude, close your eyes and see yourself looking at the most magnificent rainbow you have ever seen. Become one with the rainbow. Hug the colors, merge with them, and play with them. Spread the rainbow colors out like a great blanket, pile up all the problems you are trying to be grateful for, wrap them up, and send them as a gift to Heaven. Watch the multicolored package soar higher and higher until it disappears. As soon as the first rainbow leaves, a new one will appear. See yourself merge with the colors, slide down the rainbow, and land in a great sea of golden Light.

Greet all the Angels waiting for you, and see the scenes of the life you desire to live on Earth bubbling up to meet you out of the golden sea. Smile and breathe and say, "I Am giving thanks for MY highest joy and good." Fly high!

Message 11

FORGIVENESS

*F*orgiveness is about opening your mind to experiencing the other person's perception of what is happening. Angels know that all humans are standing in their correct places, seeing through the filters of their own lives. The valley looks deep and far away from the mountain precipice, and the precipice looks high and formidable from down inside the valley. We are here to help you to see and feel from all sides and depths, both from the selfish and selfless, from the righteous and the worthless.

We ask you to practice the experience called forgiveness by remembering to treasure your own precious divine self. Mother Father God loves you from a place of inexhaustible comfort and compassion. God wants to change how critical, judging, and inflexible humans are with themselves, and so God offers Divine Love in the vibration of forgiveness to calm you and show you another way. When you are held in the hands of God, in the hands of love, we see you begin to feel secure, and gradually you begin to let go of comparing yourself to others.

As you allow forgiveness to enter, you will transform feelings of being cheated, beaten up and neglected by another, or by yourself, or by Mother Father God.

To live with an unburdened heart, humans must first forgive themselves for abusing their own sacred temple—the physical, mental, emotional, and spiritual vessel you call you. As you are made from God and in the image of God, how can you be any less than God?

Second, humans need to forgive God for sending them to Earth to experience duality, fear, and separation from Heaven. You are here as brave healers and warriors to transform Earth back to its original destiny, and we do know how very difficult your work is. Mother Father God asks your forgiveness and for your courage to complete the re-creation of the garden of Heaven. When you remember who you are and what your mission here is all about, you can never hurt another for you have stopped hurting yourself. Welcome to forgiveness, carry it within you always, and wear it on your sleeve wherever you may go.

I Forgive You

Breathe in violet Light and exhale all fear and negativity in your body. See yourself looking at yourself naked in a long mirror. Invite the violet Fire of forgiveness to pour from the top of your head (from your own crown chakra) and pour down into the image of yourself reflected in the mirror. See yourself turn completely purple and say to your vulnerable, naked self, "I forgive you." Feel the new divine self in the mirror walk through the looking glass and merge with your heart. Invite all who need your forgiveness to meet you in the mirror. Wash away your hurt as you wash away their blindness, deafness, and unfeelingness. Say again and again, "I forgive you." Violet is the color of forgiveness, and you are the essence of love! Blessings fair beauty, sweet precious Child of God.

Message 12

ONE GOD

*H*uman beings seem to enjoy pointing out ways where they are different from one another. Some believe their way of living life is the correct way for everyone. Some desire that everyone know God through their beliefs and values, and some understand that finding God is a most personal experience.

We of the Angelic Kingdoms are truly optimistic that you will be brave enough to walk your own path home to God. One God, one Mother Father, has infinite capability to love you and only you, while completely loving all the other inhabitants of family Earth at the same time.

We encourage you to look for God's face in the rainbow of color found in the faces of Earth's children, the diverse panorama of yellow, white, brown, black, and red. Listen to their rich voices, all telling many different stories of how God lives. You are brother or sister to every human being living on Earth; when you stumble across someone homeless—in mind, body, or spirit—remember that everyone is homeless until all human beings are safely nestled back home with God.

And when you see another face of God struggling with pain or poverty of any kind, reach down to the God force in your Soul and shower that face with loving-kindness. Pay attention to where you are walking and to what Mother Father is teaching you on your journey home to God. It requires tremendous courage to acknowledge that Divine Love is taught through many vehicles, through many teachers, and we ask you to voice your name for God in your own language.

Whether you arrive home to your center crying or laughing, running or in a wheelchair, your Mother Father will greet you with open arms and a full banquet for your celebration. Find your path, follow your truth, and know that one God loves you always, with infinite grace.

God's Smile

Breathe in deeply and exhale slowly. Close your eyes, and see your face as bright and smiling. See yourself walking through a very busy international airport, smiling at each person, with a very contagious smile. See your smiling face telling everyone you meet, "I Am one with God and so are you." Close your eyes and send your happy expression to all the countries of the world.

Open your eyes and do your best to smile as often as possible, at your own reflection in the mirror, and at everyone you meet today.

Message 13
IN GOD'S TIME

*W*hen you pray for yourself or a loved one to break free from limiting patterns of thought or action, we give you our promise your prayer will manifest at the time and in the way that is for the highest joy and good of all concerned.

Each individual Soul carries perfectly orchestrated time points of exactly when the human personality will open and maintain a conscious awareness of its God potential. Awakening is a process of initiation and activation, atom by atom, cell by cell. Your process, the ignition and blazing of your Fire, is intricately woven with the process and progress of all. If you could see humanity from our perspective, you would see a pulsing Light made of tiny sparkling sparks of Fire of all colors. Divine timing is understanding and accepting the synchronicity of the Universe, all the fiery sparks igniting right on schedule. You create a brighter spark every time you allow God, expressed by your own Soul, to be in charge.

Manifestation of your prayers is dependent upon the awakening of the whole human family and by your individual desire to know and love your divine self more completely. Angels and Mother Father God hear your each and every prayer, and we ask you to find your divine will and know all requests are answered in God's time. Remember that because Mother Father God sees the big picture of your life, often you may experience something better than you prayed for.

 Time to Awaken

Breathe in slowly and exhale deeply. Close your eyes and see someone you love, someone you are concerned about, sleeping soundly on a cozy violet bed. The thick blankets of violet Fire are pulled up over the loved one's head, and you can even hear the person snoring. Call on the Angel Gabriel, and she will appear with huge gold cymbals. She will hand you a set of beautiful crystal bells, and together you will give the wake-up call. Hear the cymbals crash together as you ring the crystal bells three times. Each time Gabriel hits the cymbals together, sparks of all different colors will flow into the covers and into the body and mind of the sleeping loved one. See the loved one's body rise up in the Light and proclaim with that person, "I Am awake!"

Make sure to do this exercise seeing yourself as the sleeping person in the bed, too!

Message 14
FREE WILL

*T*he will of the ego is called free will. Free will gives the illusion that the ego is completely free to do whatever the mind chooses.

Free will can be transformed into God's will, the will of your heart at any moment. In truth, God's will has authority over free will because Mother Father God knows that misdirected free will causes you to run in circles. If you decide to jump off a cliff during a moment of despair and if it is God's will for your Soul to stay on Earth, someone will intervene in your free-will choice to die.

Willpower is about choice, instinctively choosing what is for your greatest good and focusing your intention to manifest what you desire. We believe you can direct your will to accomplish anything. Trading in free will for the will of God allows you to conquer all obstacles on your path to freedom of body, mind, heart, and spirit. God's will sets you free to create the life that your heart united with your mind chooses to live. When the choices you make come from your center instead of from a place of fear, you will attract wonderful opportunities to experience life's greatest treasures.

We believe in you and know you are willing to receive your freedom. To allow God's will to be your free will, say, "I surrender the will of my ego to the will of God."

 The Grandest Kingdom

Breathe out completely and breathe in slowly. Repeat until you feel calm and focused. See yourself sitting on an exquisite violet throne, together with the Divine Child that lives within your heart. You both have many rings of gold and silver on your fingers. Look through a doorway at your grand kingdom and see all of your hopes and dreams coming to life for you. Feel your deep satisfaction, peace, and harmony radiating out into your kingdom. Both you and your Divine Child trust that you are using your God power for the highest joy of all. Breathe in your joy and say, "I Am surrendering all I want and all I desire to God's will."

Message 15

FACING
YOUR SHADOW SELF

*F*ear's aspects of negative thinking, low self-worth, and envy are often given credit for destroying what is good and joyous. We are here to teach you that fear is your greatest teacher. The human Soul is born without fear, although it retains memory of what separation looks like and feels like. When the human Soul arrives on Earth, it is wrapped in an energy field or blanket of Mother God's Light and music. This Soul's energy of love is so magnetic and compassionate, it can attract a blanket of fear's illusion as it enters into the Earth's vibration to love and to transform. The older the Soul, meaning the more lifetimes spent on Earth, the more courage the Soul holds within. We ask old Souls to attract thick and dense layers of fear when incarnating on Earth, and transform these layers back into love.

The shadow self is the blanket of fear's negative energy your Soul agreed to learn from and eventually transform. It is this condensed layer of fear that separates the ego from Mother Father God. Your shadow is willing to be dissolved by love as soon as you recognize fear as illusion. Ask to meet your shadow and become its friend. Shadow has many secrets, for really your shadow knows exactly where you are stuck in your inhibitions and insecurities. When you feel brave enough to change and break through your attachments and all the fears you resist, your shadow will reveal all you need to see about what imprisons your ego self. When the ego knows with thought, emotion, and action that it is one with God, you are free!

Why does shadow want to tell you what you are in the dark about? Shadow is really God's energy feeling disconnected and lost, and shadow wants to come home to the Light and Sound of Divine Love. When you become aware of how shadow tricks you, then you are ready to face fear and clean all the sticky gum of self-sabotage off

the bottom of your shoes. When your shoes are clean, your Soul is
ready to race ahead and bring you your greatest destiny. Shadow has
the key. Shadow knows all.

 ### *Purple Pie*

See yourself sitting in the dark. Take a deep breath, and welcome
your shadow self to come forth from every place inside your mind.
Ask the question, "Shadow, what gift of insight do you have for me?
Why did I sabotage myself here in this situation? Why am I afraid to
try this or that?" Enjoy having a talk with your shadow self. After you
are finished talking to your shadow, it is time for shadow-shrinking.
Visualize a cream pie made of violet Fire. Say, "Thank you, shadow!"
Throw the cream pie in shadow's smirking face (looks like yourself in
a dark shadow) and feel your confidence soar as you are filled with
the delicious and sweet taste of Mother Father God's violet Fire of
transformation and forgiveness.

Message 16

TRUST

*D*o you remember the day Angel Gabriel delivered your Soul to Earth? You were asked to leave the Angels' heavenly cocoon of unconditional love to be a brave warrior for peace on Earth. Your Soul emerged on Earth to discover a brand new environment where love is given when the conditions suit the giver. When you took form as a vulnerable baby, you naturally looked to your human mother and father for the same quality and infinite quantity of love you experienced in Heaven.

Soon you discovered that your Earth parents were not capable of heavenly loving because they had forgotten what the love of Mother Father God feels like. Losing trust in God begins with losing trust in your human family because they are not emotionally and physically available to you at all times. When you were unable to change your outer world to match the Heaven you just left, you started to question if God is real.

Now is the moment to experience that Mother Father God's Divine Love exists here on Earth just as it does in Heaven. Call on your Guardian Angels at all times and in all situations. Ask us to present you with tangible evidence; miracles *can* happen in your mundane world. As you see your prayer requests answered, trust in God returns. Angels are like the hands and arms of Mother Father God, and each time you invite us into yourself, we flood your whole vessel with unconditional love.

As you experience miracles of divine intervention in your daily life, we believe it is likely you will call on us more often. We are hopeful prayer will become as automatic as breathing, and before humanity knows it, Divine Love will feel secure and dependable.

Peach Light Serenity

Close your eyes and breathe in slowly and deeply. Focus your attention on feeling your heartbeat. See yourself suspended in an enormous ball of peach Light, the energy of serenity and satisfaction. Continue to focus on listening to your heart, and roll around in the peach Light, as you feel the ball sail gently through space. See your worries look like black spots and bring them into the peach Light. Watch the black spots dissolve in the healing energy of serenity. Take a few moments to enjoy traveling around the Universe in the peach ball of Light. Breathe in the peach Light of trust and see it fill every cell of your body until you are completely united with the peach energy. This is your spiritual aura and this reunion supports you in living life unencumbered, and with an open and trusting heart.

Message 17

WALKING ON WATER

*W*hich would you choose, a gravel path or a flowing river to walk on? You would probably choose the gravel path because it appears solid and familiar. You are in control of where you are going because you have walked on the path before. Humans are trained to take control and stay in control by keeping their surroundings feeling safe and familiar. Life will feel secure only if plans are made for the future and the future looks like the past.

We of the Angelic Kingdoms do not understand why humans wish to carry their past with them into their future. From our perspective, we hope you will always be open to receiving more joy and more love. Why not enjoy something new and delightful and fulfilling each moment of your day? Angels will always choose to set down the soles of our feet in the flowing river of living in the moment.

Would you like to walk with us on the holy waters of faith? You will soon discover no control, anxiety, or manipulation is needed. Effortlessly, you will move with the flow and have no need to see where you are going. Faith is trusting that you are exactly where you need to be, experiencing all that is for your greatest good and expansion as a Child of God.

Walking on the water of faith is scary at first because you feel so light when the gravity of your past is gone. Come and experience. We will never let go of your hands. We will totally support you, and gradually as the controlling thoughts of your ego mind dissolve in faith, you simply won't imagine traveling through life any other way.

Dancing on the Holy Waters of Faith

Breathe in deeply and exhale slowly. See yourself filling boxes with all of your old concepts of how life is supposed to be lived. Pack your boxes with your family secrets and codependent trappings.

Pack up your thoughts of separation and inferiority and superiority. Pack up your addictions and attachments, and pack up all your worries about your future. Pack them all up and tie them with a golden cord of Light. Merlin arrives with his pickup truck of violet Fire (God's Light of transformation and forgiveness), and helps you carry all your boxes to the river of faith. He helps you throw the boxes into the fast-moving golden Light stream.

Watch them dissolve and when the last one is in, call on your Angels and dance upon the holy waters of faith. Say, "I Am the miracle of faith!"

Messsage 18
MANIFESTATION

*E*arth is like an enormous stage where you can act out all the experiences you need to expand your human consciousness. Your OverSoul is writing the screenplay of your outer reality every moment. All your experiences are designed with perfect accuracy and synchronicity to allow you to see and feel where you are giving away your God power. Your outer reality works like a mirror by reflecting back to you where you still believe you are separate from God. As you expand your whole self, humanity expands and each human Soul gradually reunites with its OverSoul, bringing Earth and Heaven together in the consciousness of the human mind.

Manifestation is using God's energy to bring your hopes and ideals into physical form. The more connected you become to your OverSoul, the easier it is for you to manifest your ideals consciously and instantly. This means having the ability to create with your heart and mind your outer experiences before they happen. Masters have lived and are present in your world who can visualize what they desire, focus their God force, and have their desire appear in their hands. Angels believe all humans have this ability, and yet we ask you to not let magic distract you. Use the magic of Divine Love to create a new world by trusting that all you desire to manifest will come about in a way that is for the greatest good and highest joy for all.

Manifestation demands responsibility to the voice of God within you. Learn to be quiet and hear this voice, and you will be much wiser about what you ask to experience here on Earth.

 ### Receiving the Gift

Breathe in deeply and exhale completely. Repeat until your breathing is calm and centered. See yourself and the child within your heart standing together under a bright white Light. The white Light is so brilliant, it is all you can see. Hold both sets of your hands up to the Light. Feel the love come inside you until you become one with each other and one with the Light of Divine Love. In your hands, hold up to the Light what you desire, and say once, "I Am giving thanks this gift manifests for me in God's time for the greatest good of all."

Message 19
MONEY

*M*oney was created by the human race as a symbol for the exchange of service. The energy of performing the service or making the material product is given a value based on the supply and demand of the service or product. We ask you to consider your worth as a Child of God. What value is your creative God force worth to you?

Angels believe your value is so great, we find it impossible to place a price tag on you. As Heaven and Earth come together again on your planet, we know you will begin to value your creative gifts as God values you. How you decide to express your God force on your planet affects the vibration or quality of energy you are exchanging with your world. Fear's hindrances of jealousy, laziness, greed, doubt, and unworthiness can affect the quality of your service, your talent, and the energy you are exchanging with another.

For example, if weapons, drugs, or slavery are being traded for money, the money received will have a value equal to death and imprisonment. If human creativity in the vibration of love, empowerment, and grace is being traded, the money received will multiply for the giver and receiver.

From our perspective, human beings give money an enormous sense of power and respect. To increase your worldly wealth, face your fears of lack of money and allow yourself to experience the generosity of the Universe. The stronger your fear of not having enough money, the more resistance you may have to receiving it and keeping the supply and demand of your money in balance. Another lesson we teach you is that needing money or not needing money, struggling financially or not struggling financially, has *nothing* to do with your value. Your value is infinite.

When you fully remember you are made of Mother Father God's Divine Love, your wealth comes with a continuous flow. You will always have enough and more of all the resources the physical world and the spiritual world have to offer. In order to fully remember your supreme worth, you are asked to let go of what your ego self is most afraid of losing. Money comes when you obey the creative calling of your Soul. It is a true and wise saying, "When you follow your heart, money follows." Open and receive.

 ### Dissolving Debt

Breathe in slowly and exhale completely. Close your eyes and see yourself gather up all your debts and place them in a boiling vat of violet Fire soup. As you stir the soup, surrender your fears of where the money to pay the bills will come from. Remember violet Fire is Mother Father God's Light of transformation. When the soup is done, the color will change to bright gold Light. Drink a cup of gold Light soup and say, "I Am worthy to receive God's abundance today."

Message 20

ENERGY IN BALANCE

*T*he human self has both male and female energy. Female energy is intuitive and receptive, and male energy is active and giving. Divine law requires that when you give of your life force, the quality of energy you give must be balanced with the quality of energy you receive.

For example, if a woman serves her partner and her family and does not nurture herself or receive equal service from her partner and family, she will lose her health, her money, her freedom, or her beauty. We ask you to consider Mother Earth as just such a woman. It is essential to continuously balance the male and female energy inside the human vessel to assist in restoring harmonious energy for Mother Earth.

Your planet needs to receive your love and nurturing to balance all the natural resources she is constantly giving. The spirit of Mother Earth is an Angel, and all Angels are Mother Father God's servants. We are constantly giving love to you, and we are constantly receiving love from God, for we are one. Invite us to help you balance your male and female energy, giving and receiving, serving and replenishing, so your sweet planet Earth can continue to share her rich harvest with you.

Supporting Balance for Self and for Earth

Breathe in slowly and completely. Exhale any stress and fear that you feel in your body. Repeat until you feel clear. See yourself as an enormous Angelic being. You are floating on your back in an ocean of ruby red Holy Spirit. Soak up Mother God's power and healing energy into your back, the female area of your vessel. When you feel completely saturated, see yourself standing up, straight and mighty, and holding Mother Earth in your hands. Send her white gold Light of Divine Love out through the front of your body, the male area of your vessel. Say, "I Am one with God, and I give thanks my energy is in balance for the greatest good of all."

❖❖❖

Message 21

EUPHORIA

*H*eaven is a majestic and beautiful place for little children to play. We invite you to come and be with us here in our home of joy. Inside the human heart chakra is a magical space, a doorway that gives you access to Heaven and to grand palaces existing all over the Universe. Heaven vibrates at a most lovely sound, a perfect set of tones always in tune with Divine Love and peace. Heaven is a dimension where love and peace and unity with all of God's Creation allow only feelings of joy and satisfaction.

Being is about Heaven, and being is about allowing yourself to believe for a moment that Heaven is a real place. Visiting here takes a little practice because you must come as a little child. You must allow yourself to be vulnerable and willing to leave behind worry and pain. Sometimes, humans cry when they first visit our home, and sometimes they feel physical pains in their hearts and dizzy in their brains. These sensations happen because the love is so great, we have to open you up so you can let our love in. The more you come and play with us, the higher you fly.

Angels find visiting Heaven works much better than drugs and alcohol for easing mental stress and emotional and physical pain. The effects last much longer, and you will discover that you return feeling incredibly rested and inspired about your earthly work and life.

Come and experience Angel magic, and allow us to show you that Heaven is a real place where you are always welcome. Yes, it is true you can visit loved ones living here with us at any time during your visit. You will learn that your loved one knows exactly what has been happening for you on Earth. We have no boundaries here. Come, we will show you how to find Heaven's door inside of you. You will feel like a new person.

Heaven's Doorway

Close your eyes, and take in three deep breaths. As you breathe, see a huge wooden door open in your heart and see yourself walk through the doorway. You enter a cozy emerald green room, and a little child waits for you. Find the child, and together look for the door in the ceiling of the bright green room. The door opens, and a gold Light streams down. Stand together in the Light, and you will be lifted up and out through the door in the ceiling. When you arrive in Heaven, say, "I Am euphoria, I Am one with Mother Father God." We are so looking forward to playing with you!

Message 22

LIVING IN
THE PROMISED LAND

*H*ave you ever noticed how much time you spend living inside your mind? Human beings are constantly analyzing thoughts and feelings, processing their process, and exploring via the mental self their relationship to nature, God, and humanity. God designed the human brain to function as an organic computer with the capacity to connect with Creation anywhere in the Universe.

Your mysterious computer has gradually shut down much of this ability in order to facilitate all your thoughts of judging yourself and comparing yourself to others. The greatest machine on Earth is preoccupied with evaluating where you are not good enough to call yourself a Child of God. Days turn into weeks and months of resisting your divine destiny because your brain is so busy with frustrated thinking because you do not have what you want. When your mind is clear, and judging, comparing, and wanting are escorted out the exit door, you will find yourself enjoying the promised land of a free mind.

We ask you to imagine what your daily life would be like if you were to stop judging yourself. When you open your mind and ask for spiritual guidance, Angels will tell you that judgment is unkind and unnecessary for your walk home to finding God. Comparing yourself to others creates competition and tells you to be like everyone else.

Angels do not understand this need for comparison because we know that you are not created to be like any other person in your world. You are the best one for the task at hand, and this task is for your greatest good or you would be doing something else. Wanting serves to tell you what you wish to create, but if you allow your wanting to control your mental self, happiness can visit only for brief moments. You always will be wanting more to feel happy. We wish to teach you how to free your mental self so that you can connect effortlessly with all people, animals, plants, rocks, and things.

We will show you how to live in the promised land of peaceful, joyful mental satisfaction. Repeat the entire process as many times a day as you like. You will quickly discover how positive your thoughts about life become.

 ### *Freeing Your Mind*

Breathe out like you are blowing up a balloon, and breathe in as deep as you can. See your entire mind fill with violet Fire, God's Light of transformation, and bright gold Light sparkles of love. Breathe out again, and breathe in deeply like it is your last breath before diving underwater. Again, see your entire mind fill with purple and gold Light of love. Say, "I Am all I Am, I Am all I need, I Am all I want, I Am one with God."

Message 23

DEATH

*D*eath of the joyful human spirit begins at birth. Spirit is the human will to live freely, and it is your spirit that resurrects you from death. It is spirit that calls and says, "Be brave and face all the murderers running rampant inside of you." How often do you attack yourself during one hour? How many times have you attracted death by seeing only the negative, only the dark, and only the fear?

Death brings transformation from one way of understanding to a higher, deeper, and broader view of life. The human Soul is immortal, and as it journeys through life, it brings birth where there has been death, and it brings clarity where there has been confusion.

Evolution is a gift of transformation, and so we ask you to welcome change for the greatest good in your lives. We ask you to stop resisting the death of the attackers of your self-esteem. All of your old concepts of belief in limitations and unworthiness and hierarchical structures are ready to die. Death is one of God's most loving miracles, for it ends suffering on all levels. We see it is not physical death that concerns humanity, it is the resistance to letting go of the fear of change that causes pain.

We are here to remind you of your immortality, and we ask you to cherish the physical, emotional, mental, and spiritual temple of God you are living in. How can you help your temple feel one with God with every breath, thought, and feeling? Resurrect your spirit and your life by stopping all the ways you destroy God's Creation of the human being. With the death of every fear comes love and bliss and life eternal.

 Cellular Transformation

Breathe out until you are empty. Breathe in until you are full. See yourself standing in a field in the southwest of the United States. Ahead of you stands a great platform, a funeral pyre for your death.

Next to the platform is a medicine bowl, a bowl as big as the Grand Canyon. Dancing and singing around the funeral pyre are your Guardian Angels and the Archangel Ezekiel, the Angel of death and transformation. Your Angels call you to walk up the steps of the platform and throw into the bowl all the memories, illusions, limiting beliefs, and parts of your human self you wish to transform.

Climb the steps, and lie down on the platform on the soft blanket of many colors. Close your eyes and say, "I Am releasing." Imagine that you totally dissolve in the Angel Fires in a rainbow of color. When the process is complete, you will see yourself standing in white Light in the middle of a beautiful garden. The medicine bowl has been transformed into a beautiful golden cup. Inside the Holy Grail is the ruby red Light, the Holy Spirit, divine essence of Mother God. Drink in the Light into your whole self, body, mind, heart, and spirit. Say, "I Am love."

You are now a brand-new temple of God.

Message 24

BEAUTY

*W*e will now tell you a story. Once upon a time, long ago, a beautiful child was born. This child was happy and loved to sing and draw colorful pictures of himself. He would give himself all different colors of hair in the drawings. He would draw himself short, tall, round, and square. He was a child of variety, and sometimes he would even draw himself as a she. He enjoyed showing his pictures to everyone he met, and each person always asked, "Who is this person?" The little child smiled and replied, "It is me, and they are all pictures of me!"

Angels love human beings because your personalities are so fantastic and can change as fast as the weather! With personality and talent, you are constantly creating new inventions, styles, menus, and ways of thinking about what you have created. Beauty is humanness, and as we look at you and love you, we see such loveliness and grace. We are optimistic we can convince you to look at your ego self as a gift from God, special and perfectly designed to illustrate Divine Love through your personality.

When you gently reassure your ego that your personality is attractive and worthy, your ego smiles like the little child in the story. The ego says, "It is me, they are all pictures of me." As you love your "me," you become integrated with your "I Am," and together you are united with God and united with your world. Allow yourself to acknowledge your beauty and your talents. Give yourself the gift of knowing that no one else can compare with you, for truly you are most beautiful.

✿ *I Am Beautiful*

Breathe in deeply, and exhale slowly. While looking at yourself in the mirror, see yourself on a stage standing under a brilliant spotlight wearing your best color. The audience is filled with faces of your authentic self and everyone is cheering for you. The applause is deafening, and as the flowers land at your feet, smile and breathe and say, "I Am so very beautiful!"

Message 25

CURING ADDICTION

*A*ddiction originates from longing to be one with God. Only Divine Love can fill your heart, Soul, and mind with completeness and joy. Humans have tried everything imaginable to fill the void created by separation from God. You have tried using drugs, work, sex, relationship, sacrifice, entertainment, money—and the list continues—of false substitutes for Divine Love. These "medicines" do not last, and so you try more of what does not work. If someone you love chooses to drink to quiet feelings inside, instead of going into judgment, look inside your own self for your own avoidance strategies. How do you escape from the nagging voice telling you about your misery, your own incompleteness? People with addictions are trying to survive their misery.

The cure for addiction is to find the courage to face the core fear, the deepest fear that drives the dependency on something external. This is the fear of abandonment. Without your fear of loss, you would be free to let your Soul guide you in the fulfillment of your heart's desires.

The Angelic detox center is always open. When you enter our home, we will fill you up with love and gently show you that you are not alone. As you remember your unity with Mother Father God, you automatically let go of chemical, material, and relationship crutches you have desperately needed. The root of your addiction comes from believing you were abandoned by Divine Love, and no earthly substance can substitute for the real thing. Curing addiction is simple because there is only one cure: Oneness with your God self.

Be brave enough to ask for our help, and we will begin our treatment of God's healing love. We are looking forward to celebrating your recovery and the recovery of all people on your planet—present, past, and future. Heaven on Earth is our promise, and Angels always keep their promises!

🌸 *Restoring You*

Breathe in deeply and exhale slowly. See yourself as a tree and your legs and feet are your roots. Ask Archangel Michael to come and cut down the tree that is you. He takes the roots and bathes them in violet Light, God's energy of transformation and forgiveness. With the upper part of the tree that is you, he places the trunk and branches in warm ruby red Light, the Fire of love and compassion from Mother God. As you feel your tree parts soaking in the colors, say these words, "I Am one with God with my whole Tree of Life." Michael will put you back together and you will then see yourself as a strong, healthy tree of gold and green Light. Imagine that the tree that is you grows up and touches the sun. See your roots growing deep in the Earth and touching the warm center of Mother Earth's heart. Allow the energy of Father Sun and Mother Earth to restore you. Once you feel strong, grounded, and peaceful, say, "I forgive myself. I love myself. I respect myself. I am grateful and happy to be reunited with my divine self, now."

Message 26
GOD'S CHILD

*F*rom the beginning, your heart has remained in the heart of your Mother Father God. As you grew from two cells into a fetus into an infant and on to an adult, loving embraces flowed from God's center into your center. Inside your heart lives a little child filled with Divine Love, and she is waiting to share all this abundance with you. Any abuse, neglect, or hardship you may have suffered throughout your life covers the little child inside your heart.

We wish to show you how to lift the cover of hurt off your heart so you can feel all the love you have been missing, all the love you have been waiting for. God's Child within your heart is a voice to your subconscious, to the past you have forgotten. God's Child is the doorway to direct communication with your OverSoul, always guiding you from Heaven.

Angels specialize in helping humans find their broken hearts, mend them, and transform them into brand new. We are here to teach you how to love the child within you as God loves you, as an only child. It is not necessary for you to revisit the past; just lift the cover, and find God's Child resting peacefully in Mother Father God's generous lap of everlasting love. Come with us. We have someone we wish you to meet. He wants to play with you and teach you about the miracles of Heaven. She knows all the dreams about your future, and she is the magic one who can make them come true for you.

 ### *Meeting the Child Within*

Take some slow and deep breaths. Close your eyes, and see yourself walk into a tunnel made of beautiful stones of all shapes and colors. The tunnel leads into an emerald green ocean of Light. As you enter the green Light, look for a coral-colored oyster shell and pop open the lid. Inside lives God's Child, the child of your heart.

God's Child might need a gentle shower with violet Fire raindrops to wash away old pain.

When God's Child is free, play and play and play in the green Light. Enjoy and do try and visit this magical Child each day. Your divine self has much to tell you!

Message 27

CLEANING HOUSE

*H*uman beings have a great storage capacity for holding onto old feelings because humans do not understand how to let go of pain. Painful emotions must be cleared from the mental and emotional bodies, or their energy will be soaked up by the cells in your physical body. It is instinctive for you to resist processing hurt feelings because you are trying to protect yourself from the fear of being hurt again.

Frequently the ego self convinces you to forget or ignore the experience, and often you continue to attract new experiences that bring up the same feelings you tried to ignore. Abandoned feelings will seep out like toxic waste until they are completely transformed into forgiveness and love. For example, when your ideas or feelings are rejected by someone you care about, this disappointment opens the vault of cellular memory of any time in your past where you felt unappreciated. Your shadow self grabs onto the hurt and sends out the belief that you will continue to experience more rejection in the future.

Unresolved painful experiences and the fear they will repeat creates separation between you and your higher self.

We desire for you to experience feelings of joy and believe your life will continue to improve and open. Knowing that Mother Father God lives within you and all around you is essential for creating Heaven's miracles in your life. We of the Angelic Kingdoms offer you our clearing services. We are efficient, courteous, and reliable and know where all the cobwebs are hiding.

 Angelic House Clearing

Close your eyes, and breathe in deeply and slowly. See yourself stepping into a bubbling pool of violet Fire. As you soak in the violet Fire, imagine your whole vessel—mental, emotional, and physical—is a giant sponge saturated with old emotion. Ask your Guardian Angel to come and wring out the sponge. When the sponge is empty, soak up more violet Fire into your every pore and again ask your Angel to wring out the sponge. Continue as long as you like, and you may find it helpful to focus on certain feelings or experiences. Once you are all clear, you will see or feel that the violet water has now changed into a white-gold color. This is the refueling energy of Divine Love. Soak up the love and start your life anew!

Message 28

LOVING YOUR PETS

*P*ets are Nature Angels devoting their lives to assisting humans in the healing of their emotional selves. Animals and plants and even inanimate pets soak up stress and fear for you, and they are constantly relaying messages from Angels and Mother Father God. Animals, both domestic and wild, work diligently to help clear and transform the negative energy generated from fearful thought into love and kindness.

City rats have a great deal of responsibility, and so we are hopeful you will send them a bit of gratitude. They absorb emotional garbage generated by wasteful thought, and discarded feelings. In comparison, the family dog and cat absorb the stress and tension in the houshold atmosphere.

Your family pets are sensitive to your thoughts and feelings, and they will mirror back to you what you might not see. For example, cats are a metaphor for feelings, as they are felines. If your cat enjoys sitting in the middle of your work papers, perhaps you need to give your feelings a little attention. When you are looking for some divine guidance from an earthly perspective, talk to your family pet, the wildlife around your neighborhood, or the animals at the zoo. Talking to animals and plants requires concentrated listening.

Your pets understand every word you speak to them, and they can hear every thought you think. They may not always choose to listen, just as you may not always choose to listen to them or to your higher self. We are delighted to have the opportunity to teach you how to communicate with the world of Nature Angels living with you and all around you. Give thanks for God's Creation, and God's Creation will show thanks to you!

Pet Talk

Sit comfortably with your pet and ask if now is a good time for a chat. The pet will give you a signal of yes or no. Send love energy straight from your heart, and feel the vibration of love that comes back. Ask your pet a question. The answer will come through in your own thought because animals communicate telepathically and most often through sending mental images. The more you practice communicating with your pet, the easier this communication becomes!

Message 29

ANGELS' KEYS TO SUCCESS

*A*ngels are successful with our work of performing miracles because we truly believe in what we are doing. We know without a doubt that we are working for the highest joy and good of all. We love our work, for it brings us great joy, and so we have nothing to complain about.

Our first key to your success is to listen to your heart at all times and follow your truth.

Our second key is to stop complaining and making excuses for why you cannot follow your heart.

Our third key is to allow yourself to receive for what you give and to ask for this exchange to be in balance.

Our fourth key is to remember that all money comes from Mother Father God and that God is the source of your paycheck.

Our fifth key is to allow yourself to express your creative talents and share God's gifts with the world.

Everyone does want what you have to share, so if you enjoy your craft, continue. If you are miserable at what you do, ask yourself why you are forcing yourself to do work that compromises your integrity.

Our sixth key is to know what you are responsible for and allow others to do their own work, even if you feel you can do a better job.

Our last key, number seven, is to ask for Angelic assistance throughout your day. For every creative concept, a **Deva** Angel is ready to help you manifest it here on Earth. Angels love to smooth out the rough edges, cut through red tape, and bring truth and justice to Light for all to see.

Serve from your heart and ask to know how your daily work contributes to humanity. When you have a sense of divine purpose, your success is certain and heavenly!

Filling with Success

Breathe out any stress in your mind and body. Breathe in loving-kindness in a soft gold Light. Mentally record all the reasons why you cannot be successful doing what your heart desires. Please include any old family beliefs or fears, and fears concerning financial support. See yourself burn the list in God's violet Fire of transformation and forgiveness and say, "I Am free to be who I Am." Now, see yourself totally immersed in a bright turquoise Light. Turquoise is the Angel Fire of success and this energy helps to release your God will-power, courage, and your worthiness. Say, "I Am fame and fortune for the greatest good of all concerned!"

Message 30

RESTORING

*H*umans have been taught for ages to sacrifice their needs for the needs, wants, and demands of others. With sacrifice comes denial of self, feelings, and connection to God. When the human self is neglected, exhaustion and eventual illness can overtake the emotional and physical bodies.

To restore your vessel, Angels recommend you begin by allowing yourself to feel. Feelings can show that you believe you are less powerful or less worthy than another. All feelings are sacred because your emotional self is directly connected to the spiritual body. Connecting to spirit solely via the masculine mind of thinking does not work efficiently. The Divine Feminine force is equally important to your planet, meaning Mother God's energy of emotion needs to balance with Father God's energy of thought on Earth. Connecting to spirit with pure thought (Divine Masculine) and clear feeling (Divine Feminine) allows you to experience the greatest healing.

In ages past, students of spiritual enlightenment could expand their intuitive ability just by thinking. Now, in the age of Heaven on Earth, all students expand by feeling their feelings and balancing emotion with intellect. Intimate Oneness with Mother Father God happens when you put God first in your daily life; this means nurturing your whole vessel by respecting your feelings.

We remind you that sacrifice and denial of feeling are natural responses for you. We are in your life to assist you in healing every aspect of yourself. Call on us, and we will show you how to allow God—through your own center—to guide you and nourish you. It is only when you are full that you can give to others. If you are empty, you have nothing to offer. We welcome you to experience Angelic restoration. It is like visiting a healing sanctuary inside yourself.

Angel Sanctuary

Begin to breathe in deeply and exhale slowly. See yourself lying on a bed of thick and soft emerald green moss. The **Cherubim** Angels come and offer you a refreshing drink from the great cup of love. Drinking the beautiful ruby energy will restore you completely with Mother God's unconditional love. Allow the green Light of healing, flowing into you from the soft green moss, and the ruby energy, Divine Mother's love, to completely saturate you inside and out. Say, "I Am soaking up love, love, and more love." Invite your feelings to come forth from deep inside you, listen, release, and restore.

Message 31
PARENTING

*T*he individual human being deserves freedom to *be*. Parenting is about creating a sacred space for children to grow and discover their God potential. Every person wants to be taken care of, to be listened to, and loved for who one is, not just for what one gives you. We ask you to remember with a compassionate heart that each person's true desire is "Please, take care of me." Whether you are the most independent and courageous person or whether you cannot leave your house without all-weather gear and a companion at your side, you want with all your heart for loving parents to take care of you and protect you.

Angels are parents who are available at all times and in all situations, for we never have headaches, and we never throw our backs out. Children of all ages need our loving parenting, and so we offer our complete devotion to you and to your family.

When you are exhausted and need comforting and a baby-sitter is nowhere to be found, call on us. We will come and support you while you care for your child. We will help you to release the stress, worry, and burden of feeling overwhelmed by life. Human parents become healthier and wiser teachers when they allow their Angels and Guides to mother and father them. We will joyously prove to you that you are not alone. All children are Mother Father God's Children, and God's love can provide all the support you need and want both spiritually and physically.

Be wise and loving parents, and give your children space to grow. Encourage them to remember that because God lives inside of them, they need to treat themselves with tremendous respect, and this goes for you, too. Enjoy being a child for your whole life and know we are protecting and loving you always!

Angel Love

Breathe in deeply and exhale slowly. Close your eyes, and see your-self curled up next to your Guardian Angel. You are resting on a lush ruby-red velvet sofa, and the pillow is just right. Breathe in the soft red color of the velvet, and feel the fabric with your hands. Say, "I Am the beloved child of Mother Father God." As you rejuvenate, you may desire to see your children come and rest with you. The ruby sofa of Mother God's Holy Spirit will grow as large as you need it to, and you will discover there is enough room for several genera-tions. Enjoy and relax and soak up the love and protection from your Angel parents!

Message 32

UNDERSTANDING VIOLENCE

*V*iolence comes from repressed anger, and anger comes from feeling cheated, rejected, abandoned, and unworthy. Angels believe anger can be your greatest emotion, for you do not make changes until you are angry. However when the human being is sad, guilty, depressed, embarrassed, or lonely, the situation is often tolerated until anger comes. Anger makes a human change inside and out. When anger is expressed in violence, serious harm can happen, and when the vibration of anger is raised to the vibration of Soul-inspired volition and action, healthy change can happen for the greatest good of all concerned.

Physical violence is a reaction to feeling powerless, and so the Twelve Archangels of the Central Soul offer you a new source of power. Trade in your weapons for Angel power, Angel energy that is all-powerful and all-loving at the same time. We suggest that when you have had all you can take, when you feel you have been a victim of another's actions for too long, ask us to help you set boundaries for yourself. Ask yourself if the situation feels at all familiar to anything you may have experienced as a child. If the answer is yes, travel with us back to your past, and wash the whole scene (until it disappears) in your mind's eye using an Angel hose that sprays God's violet Fire of transformation and forgiveness.

As you let the purple Light flood the memory, the past is transformed into love and freedom for your present. If the situation is one you are struggling with now, again spray the violet Fire cleansing water on all people you have allowed to violate your sacred space. Using the color purple to clear painful experiences supports instant transformation. When you use violet Fire to clear another person, the energy automatically clears your vessel of negative energy too. Angel energy is love, and love heals all hurts. You will see immediate changes in your outer world, and you will feel free from past traumas you continue to carry with you.

Freedom is yours. Don't just react to violence of body, mind, heart, and spirit. Do something about it!

 ### Releasing Trauma

Breathe in slow and deep. Exhale gently. Repeat until you feel calm. Close your eyes, and see in front of you a large paint bucket filled with purple Light, and a paintbrush ready to spread this violet Fire. You also have on hand Archangel Michael's sapphire blue laser of Light that pierces through illusion and allows truth and awareness to shine through. Think of someone you are angry with, someone who has hurt you, and you have not been able to entirely release the experience. Paint the person who hurt you with violet Fire until he or she dissolves in the Angel energy of transformation and forgiveness. Imagine the scene of the past is a painting and pierce it with Michael's sapphire laser until you feel your chest open and expand. Keep breathing, and as you let go of the past that haunts you, say, "I Am free. I Am safe. I Am protected and I choose to live!" When you feel complete, ask your higher self and your Angels how to set healthy boundaries for yourself in the future. Welcome to freedom and welcome to love!

Message 33

FALLING IN LOVE
WITH YOURSELF

*O*n the day we met, I fell in love with you. I am your Angel, and I am your Guide and protector. When you connect with me and give me thanks, it is your higher self that you discover. Human beings and Angels, and loving kind people you meet on your path home, all reflect back to you the love bursting inside your heart, the love you feel for you. Heaven sings with you with each opening of your heart. As you open yourself to falling in love with another, with God, and with life, Heaven and Earth come a little closer.

We are delighted to assist you in falling in love every moment of your day. The euphoric feelings tell us you are beginning to understand who God is and who you are. Celebrate the sacred marriage between you and your heart, and love will continue to find you.

To create a fairy tale come true, first fall in love with *you*; then your prince, princess, king, or queen must come, for it is divine law. Oneness is a precious discovery and when you open your heart to yourself and then to another, Oneness happens. Be brave, and ask us to help you create Oneness with your own mind, heart, body, and Soul, and then true bliss is yours when you meet your divine companion.

Never settle for less than what you deserve—true love, truest love. Look for your beauty reflected in the eyes of all you admire and know I am your Angel, and together we are celebrating forever.

 Emerald and Gold Fusion

Breathe out any fear in your body and breathe in love. Close your eyes, and see your heart sending out the luscious emerald green Light of love. Allow the love to flow until you are immersed in the green Light. From above your head, the bright golden white Light of Divine Love begins to flow and swirl with the love Light of your heart. Say, "I Am Oneness. I Am Oneness. I Am Oneness."

Enjoy—and remember, true love is worth waiting for.

Message 34

MOTHER AND FATHER

*I*nside your center lives God. God is both Mother (Divine Emotion) and Father (Divine Thought). When you are completely connected to your Divine Mother and Father, you can fully express the power and love of God in your daily life on Earth. We of the Angelic Kingdoms believe that now is the time for humanity to think and feel from the heart center. To raise the vibration of your thoughts to their highest purity, begin by paying attention to what you are thinking.

When negative or fearful thoughts come crusading into your conscious awareness, infuse them with violet Fire and transform them into love. To open to the liberating power of Divine Emotion, we ask you to have the willing intention to feel your feelings without judgment or negative reaction. The higher power of emotion, together with pure thought, keeps you in your heart center, the place of trust, faith, and Oneness with the Universe.

As you learn to live from your heart, you learn how to become your own loving mother and father. We will teach you how to clear out old male (thought energy) and old female (emotional energy) to make room for the Divine. Enjoy your new awareness, and remember that joy is contagious. We see you sharing your new positive attitude with all you meet. Freedom and continuous joy are yours when you think and feel from your holy heart space.

In the following imagery exercise, we use a wardrobe or closet as a symbol for what is lost or hidden in your consciousness. Sleeping men symbolize old negative and limiting thought patterns and worn out concepts of how life is to be lived. Sleeping women and children are metaphors for repressed emotions and absorbed emotions originating from other people. Cleaning the closet with Angel energy represents release of the old and fulfillment with Divine Love.

Wardrobe Clearing

Breathe in deeply and exhale slowly. See yourself transform into an enormous wardrobe with doors on both the front and back. Open the door to the front, and look inside for sleeping men. They may look sick or weak or miserable. In your hands you are holding a fireman's hose that sprays violet Fire. Spray all the men with purple Light of transformation and forgiveness. Keep spraying until the wardrobe is completely clear. Now, imagine walking around to the back of the closet and opening the door. This time, you have a floodlight of ruby red Fire, and when you shine the Light on any sleeping, depressed, or sick women or children, they will disappear in the Holy Spirit, the healing Light of Mother God's love. Continue until the back of the wardrobe is completely clear, and say, "I welcome my Divine Mother and Father to live fully within me." Take three deep breaths and say, "We are one, I Am one with Mother Father God."

Message 35

MEETING
YOUR GUARDIAN ANGELS

*G*uardian Angels work constantly to open your heart, your mind, and the vision of your life. The human potential amazes us, and we are determined to bring you to your highest and most joyful potential. We are within you and all around you, reminding you that you are a Child of God. We speak to you in the occurrences, events, and happenings of your mundane world. Everywhere you look, you can find an Angelic message of wisdom right under your nose. We teach you with your outer world, and we teach you through the faces and life experiences of all that you encounter.

Angels are devoted to helping humans on their journey, and so we call you to open your minds, hearts, and vessels to our love. When you call for our assistance, we respond!

The human self is not in control, and often we show you that relief comes in God's time and in God's way of manifestation. Guardian Angels help you surrender control to trusting and having faith. We are here to remind you, as often as needed, God keeps you safe and provides for all you need.

We recommend you do not spend your quiet time trying to see us or hear us speak to you in long conversations. We tell you to discover us by opening your life to results, to long-awaited changes, and actions for your greatest good. When fear comes to visit, breathe and know we are present. Face your fear and let go of what you are afraid of losing. Surrender to God's love and listen for the steps to resolve the problem. Your divine self will direct you. Watch as your reality changes, and once again all is well. Angels are not on Earth to bring happiness in the way your ego expects it to appear. Ego's expectation is often far too limited compared with what you can receive with your heart. We are here to remind you to live from your heart and to focus on the present moment.

Living in the present, without clinging to the past or constantly predict-ing the future, will bring you eternal joy and freedom. Come, we will show you!

 Angel Embrace

Close your eyes and breathe. See a luscious gold Light gently swirl-ing around you, lifting you up, and filling you with love. Allow this gold Light to wash away any sticky negative thoughts or resentments from your day. Open and say, "Guardian Angels, I Am ready to play." Remember, we are Light and music, and we answer in action. Just be with us and know we are real! Tell us what you desire, what you need, and where you need comfort. Breathe and feel us connecting with you, loving you as you have never been loved before!

Message 36

LAW OF ATTRACTION

*S*omething quite miraculous happens when you allow yourself to experience life from your heart center. The heart center is the home of God within you, and as you live from this house, life flows with peaceful serenity. How can life on Earth possibly stay calm and joyful?

The house of God inside your heart has doors and windows impervious to fear and to attachment. Debt and pain and hurt cannot enter this home, although the solutions are often found just inside the doorway, just inside the windowsill.

As Children of God, you have the power to bring to you all you need, and this is the divine Law of Attraction. We will show you how to work with the law, and you will need to surrender control. Control stops the magic.

When you are ready for your prayer to be answered, you will attract the experience, relationship, circumstances, career opportunity, or assistance right into your energy field, up close and personal.

When you are not ready, but your ego believes you are, you can try to force what you want by beating the pavement, the bushes, the diner, and even the heavens, and you will still not be ready. Surrendering the timing of receiving what you have asked for is another lesson you will learn when living in the home of God. Resistance to surrendering to God's will creates inner and outer conflict. You will continue to learn that God always wins, and ego control always lets go in the end. Angels are present to show you what you are truly ready to attract into your human experience, for often it is wonderful and will bring you great joy. Together, breaking through your resistance to surrendering and attracting, effortlessly, the miracles you are ready for can make for a very satisfied human being. Attract from your divine self and experience the feeling of home, sweet home.

Truth

See yourself standing in a rain shower of Archangel Michael's sapphire blue Light of truth. Invite the blue Light to wash away all the entrapments your ego and shadow self have led you to believe about your life. See the blue Light fill your throat and wash through your whole body. Ask for the miracle of speaking your truth, feeling your truth, knowing your truth and living your truth. Watch the resistance to being your most authentic self flow down the drain with the dirt and the soap bubbles, and say, "I attract, effortlessly, all I need to live my most joyful life, now."

Message 37

BELIEVING IN MIRACLES

*E*xperiencing miracles requires trusting your Angels are listening at all times and in all situations. A miracle may not always suit your ego's expectations. Do you realize that every good failure is actually a miracle in disguise? It all depends on how you choose to understand and deal with the disappointment. When your goals are for your greatest good, they manifest in God's time and in God's way. If the great success that you dreamed of turns to dust before your eyes, we say to you—watch the dust!

Watch and see what creative passions and new directions spring up from the death of what was not meant to be and embrace the miracle that is being born from the loss. From our perspective, the ego often seeks the easy road and the easy road is an empty road. Soul says to choose the road that challenges your comfortable routines because this is the road blessed with miracles and prosperity. With every challenge, Mother Father God blesses you with a miracle to overcome the challenge, to learn from it and to evolve. You are here to express the creativity and passions of your Soul and it is through Soul, not ego, that you are guided to greater success and happiness. Ego does not like change because ego wants to feel safe and in control, and control blocks the flow of receiving God's miracles of blessings and abundance.

The ego may or may not recognize that it is afraid of being real and true—however, Soul knows. Soul calls out to the Guardian Angels and to the Twelve Archangels of the Central Soul and says, "Angels, we have a stubborn one here!" The Angels respond immediately by orchestrating miracles of help, new opportunities, and what appears to the ego as good luck. We ask you to love your ego and be compassionate because ego is afraid of the unknown and constantly feels inadequate. It is what ego does and this is why miracles will always come when you need them most, no matter what mood or frame of mind ego is in.

Let go of what the miracle may look like or where it might come from. Just believe that you are totally and completely loved by Divine Oneness.

Your Angels will never let you down. Let go, surrender, and believe even when your ego doesn't want to believe. Oh, and do ask for a miracle when you want or need one. It is safe to ask. You cannot block a miracle, ever. God sends them to you and God *is* in charge.

 Dancing in Heaven

Breathe out and in. With the out breath, say "Fear out." With the in breath, say "Love in." Continue breathing and reciting, "Fear out, love in," until you feel less anxious. See yourself walk through a big purple door and enter into a luscious emerald green pasture. See and feel the **Butterfly Angels** dancing around you. See their faces and gorgeous multicolored wings, feel their soft kisses on your cheeks, and hear their delightful laughter in your ears.

Dance with them and dance with the little Child of God that lives within your heart. Breathe out fear and breathe in love and feel the magic of Heaven. Say, "I believe in miracles. I believe in love. I believe in me." Enjoy!

Message 38
SHABUNGI SOS

*P*lanet Earth is a place where human beings come to learn how to take responsibility for what they think and for what they do and feel. Humans create their experiences with thought and emotional energy. **Shabungi** is negative or low vibration energy that is made from thought and powered with emotion. What most human beings do not know is that low vibrations travel to a higher vibration in order to neutralize. This means that if one person does her work to keep her mind clear of negativity, pays attention to her feelings and deals with them, then she may become a shabungi magnet. She can attract all of the negative vibrations for hundreds, sometimes thousands, of miles away!

Shabungi is also absorbed into Mother Earth as she is a living being and a great Angel. A person with a higher vibration than the spot on which he stands can pull the shabungi right out of the Earth into his own vessel. Animals also absorb shabungi and pets absorb shabungi for their owners. We do not recommend being in denial that these low vibrations are all around you because they do contribute to illness of your mental, emotional, and physical bodies. Instead, we ask that you *wake up to shabungi* and pay attention to the thoughts running through your mind. Pay attention to what you are feeling in your body because this is where emotion communicates. For example, anger can increase your pulse and heart rate. Sadness can make you feel sleepy and tired. Happiness can give you energy and peacefulness can dissolve knots in your muscles and make that nagging headache go away.

As you become more aware of your own thoughts and feelings, you will begin to become aware of the vibrations of the people around you as well as the places you visit. Love transforms low vibration into higher vibration and love that comes without conditions helps to transmute shabungi for the entire planet. We encourage every human being to cleanse the negative thoughts out of your mind and when you are in fear, breathe it out, and focus on *love*. When you are feeling angry, guilty, obsessed, anxious, sad, resentful, or lazy, then focus on where you feel the contraction in your physical body and breathe love into this area until you feel the contraction let go and your breathing return to normal. By staying aware, you give great service to humanity and each time an Angel sees you trying to clear shabungi from your own vessel or from an area, tens of thousands of Angels, Devas, and Nature Spirits step in to help you!

We thank you for clearing the shabungi pollution where you sense it! We thank you for your service. We thank you for making planet Earth healthier for all concerned.

Clearing Shabungi

Please begin by paying attention to what you are feeling in your body. Do you feel contracted in your breathing? Is there any area of your body that feels tight or stressed? See your entire body fill up with violet Fire, the energy of transformation and forgiveness. See the violet Fire flow out of your feet, palms of your hands, and top of your head. Keep focusing on the color purple until all you can see and feel is violet Fire. When your thoughts are negative, whining, or fearful, ask your Angels to send you a violet Fire tidal wave of love and see the wave flush all of the shabungi out of your head and body. Say, "I choose love!" Allow the tidal wave of violet Fire to flood the entire space where you are and stretch far beyond and include your town, county, state, country, and the world.

❖❖❖

Message 39

LOVE AND MARRIAGE

*H*uman beings develop most effectively through intimate relationship. It is creating a partnership—based on love and friendship—that allows the wounded child and self to come out from hiding under the cellar stairs. "Finally there is someone to love me," cries the child within! And then the wounded child says, "But what if you hurt me like I have been hurt before, or neglect me or abandon me? I had best create this hurt, neglect, and abandonment so that I get it over with because this is what I am used to. This is what I deserve." Angels and Guides in Heaven are very aware of how partnership works on Earth, and we say to you, the deeper and more unconditional the love is between two people, the greater the healing! Love, shared consistently and without judgement, accelerates the surfacing of the deepest wounded child beliefs. Both partners will need to be supportive of one another when any of these beliefs, such as unworthiness to be loved, fear of abandonment, loss of control, and expectations of rejection rise to the surface.

We are not saying that all people will marry or that all people should marry. We are saying that there is a person for you to love and who will love you in return if you will allow this person to come to you. You deserve the healing because with the healing of the wounded child comes success and happiness. There is no way to avoid the purging of the old beliefs facilitated by real love, unless you pack your bags and run. Sadly, this is what many people choose to do when they have finally found true love and all of a sudden realize that their beloved partner is reminding them of their own mother or father. We say, "Exactly!" The child within you needs your love, attention, acknowledgment, and affection. If you do not have it for your own child, then you do not have it to give to a partner and vice versa. Fill up with the Divine Love of Mother Father God. Open your vessel to the great energy of the Central

Sun. Your Creator always has replenishing love for you. The more that you receive love from Source, then the more you have for the little child within you, and the more you have for your partner. Be prepared for some projection of your parents onto the one you love, and thank him or her for what he or she reflects back to you. Let the old lies and hurt go back to God and open to receive more love, awareness, and happiness every day.

We do not recommend comfortable marriages where it is easy to fall asleep and exist as causal friends coexisting together under the same roof. Instead, we encourage you and your partner to embrace growing and evolving *together*. Please stay full of Divine Love so that your relationship is overflowing with passion, affection, companionship, mutual respect, and understanding.

 Welcome to the Twelve Archangels Marriage Counseling

Breathe out any anger, resentment, or frustration you are feeling for your beloved. Breathe in love and gratitude. See yourself enter through a beautiful purple door into the emerald green field of your heart. Look around and feel the *unconditional* love. Find the Child of Divine Love that lives within your heart and ask him or her to bring to you all of the hurting little children hiding within your vessel. Call on your Divine Feminine and Divine Masculine as well as any Angels, Guides, and loved ones now living in Heaven. Say, "I allow you, *all of you,* to love *me*." Keep repeating this until all of the hurt children dissolve in the love and merge with the Divine Child. Now you are ready to invite your partner and his or her little child into your heart. Send true love to your partner and child, and open and receive their love as it flows back to you.

Message 40

RESOLVING CONFLICT

*I*nner conflict between the ego and Soul or between ego and the heart often manifests in your outer reality as a problem to resolve with someone else. You also may discover your inner conflict reflected in another's issue and wonder why you have such a strong desire to rescue your friend and fix the problem.

Resolving conflict always asks that you look inside yourself to find the root cause of the problem. Where is your ego in conflict with your Soul? Does your Soul pull you to share your gifts with the world while ego wants to stay home and hide under the covers? Where is your ego in conflict with your heart? Does your ego want to be in control and be right while your heart is telling you to forgive and surrender? When you are having a conflict with another person, the wisest thing to do is to ask: "What do I need to change in *my* life?" It could be as simple as that you do not want your energy to go into feeding drama. Some human beings thrive on drama while others do not. Angels do not judge drama as good or bad. We see that some of you enjoy playing out your internal issues with others, and some of you prefer to process alone.

Whether you tolerate more or less crisis in your life, we ask, "Are you a natural problem solver or a problem maker?" Either way, you are trying to resolve something that is troubling you with *you*. Often the person who creates problems does so because the wounded child within is desperate for attention and wants to be noticed. The person who is the problem solver is likely to have a wounded child within that wants to be needed, and here again he or she is seeking attention and desires to be noticed and feel valued. So whether you make the problem or solve the problem, conflict shows you a wounded child seeking love. The wounded child is your subconscious and your subconscious rules the ego from underground. When the wounded child is heard and loved then your ego feels safe and automatically surrenders to your heart and Soul.

We do hope that you are seeing the great importance of conflict in your life, even if it doesn't happen often in your own life, but is reflected in the lives of those around you. We ask you to pay attention and be aware of your feelings and take a moment to love the hurting child within. Unconditional love brings resolution to all internal conflicts. Once the conflict is resolved within you, it often can be settled through open and honest communication with the other person. If the other person is unwilling to take responsibility for her feelings or behavior, surrender her to the Angels' care. Most important, the more you listen to your feelings and take full responsibility for them, the fewer problems you will experience in your everyday life.

 Conflict Resolution

Breathe deeply. Breathe out fear and breathe in love until you feel calm and centered. Feel the conflict in your gut, and mull it over in your mind. See yourself write a title for your conflict on a blackboard. Title the conflict. Include the subject of the disagreement and the names of those involved. Now, add the key words describing how you feel on the blackboard. Take an eraser made of violet Fire and erase all of your feelings and thoughts about the conflict. Keep watching until the answer for resolving the conflict appears on the blackboard.

Message 41

THE LAW OF INSIDE OUTSIDE

*W*elcome to learning how to use the ancient magic of school-room Earth. Everything that you need to pass through each test and move higher in consciousness is right in front of you. Human beings create their reality with their thoughts and beliefs and when it is time for an old lie to die, you can be sure that it will present itself to you through your environment, just like magic.

Let's say that you need to find employment, but you do not know which direction to take. Well, you can be sure that someone will appear in your life who describes exactly what you need to do for work. You may not recognize it immediately, especially if the ego is resisting the obvious. Let's say that you have a gift as a writer but you have not been writing due to various distractions and reasons. This ancient magic works by your Soul bringing into your life exactly what Soul needs you hear. In our example, this would manifest as a friend calling on the phone and saying, "Guess what, I feel a push to start writing again."

The Law of Inside Outside can work in reverse: you might be tempted to find work that you have outgrown and no longer serves your heart and Soul. In this case, you may very well attract someone who offers you a job doing the old job, or who tells you that he was just hired to do the work that you outgrew. The feeling inside of you will be one of repulsion, as your Soul will reject the past with a strong negative feeling in your gut. We ask that you take a look at what is happening or not happening for you. Go within and see what you are feeling inside of your body. Listen to the thoughts running through your head. Do these thoughts and feelings feel and sound like the past? If yes, then you are living in your past inside your mind and something is happening on the outside, in your environment, that looks and feels just like it did in the past. When your thoughts and feelings make you feel happy and hopeful, you can be sure you are obeying the calling of your Soul.

Although most human beings find it difficult to *see* their hidden subconscious beliefs, we say to you: Wake up and smell the roses or the cow dung. Either way, your inner beliefs are communicating through your outer reality.

Pay attention and you can immediately change what brings you sorrow into what feels good and true both inside and out.

 ### What Is Missing?

Breathe in Divine Love in the colors white and gold. Exhale any frustrations or anxiety held within your body. Focus on your breathing and when you feel centered, ask, "What is missing in my outer reality?" Is it love and affection? Is it money and career advancement? Is it good health and vitality? Say, "I Am willing to experience the miracle of my Angels and Guides showing me through my everyday life what I need to change on the inside in order for the outside to change for the better. I *allow.*"

Message 42

ANGELS' WINGS

*A*ngels' wings are made of Divine Love and protect you at all times and in all situations. Angels cannot interfere in your lessons or with your karma; however, we can guide you through your intuition and move you left, right, up, and down with our energy. Our wings are alive and all-powerful. Every moment of every day the wings of Angels touch each and every human being and believe it or not, humans can see Angel wings. Although they see them, they do not acknowledge their presence unless they choose to do just this. Take a moment while you read this and look out of the corners of your eyes. You will see us. We are here. If you believe you do not see us, it is because your mind is expecting something different from what your eyes see. Our wings look like pulsing white Light unless we feel like showing you our colors.

When an Angel stands directly facing you, your brain prevents you (unless you have learned to trust) from seeing the great Being of Light and Sound showering you with Divine Love and affection. Why is this? Because you might think that you have gone batty, or convince yourself that you made up the image in your imagination. Humans feel safest when they see what vibrates at the same wavelength as their own bodies. All things in physical manifestation on the Earth share a similar vibration and this is why you see people, plants, furniture, and other things as tangible and sensible. When an Angel's wing touches you, you can be sure the Angel has an important message to deliver. Yes, God is talking, and God's Angels are the messengers. Your ego might not always like the message; however, your ego, heart, body, and Soul need the message.

Do Angels hear you? Yes, Angels hear your every thought, positive or negative. We tell you that we hear your prayers even before you have said them. We see you. We feel you. We touch you. We protect you. We *love you.* Ask to experience the feeling of our embrace.

Angels' Wings

See yourself standing in Heaven's doorway. Look for a purple door that opens your mind to your heart and to Heaven. Breathe in love and open the door. Walk through and look for us in the flower garden. You do not need to fear us. We are made of loving-kindness, and our joy expands when we help you. Breathe in our joy and ask us to appear. Do you see us? Keep breathing and allow your brain to show you what your heart sees all the time: Angels' wings surrounding you. One or more Angels, great Beings of Light and Sound, will walk up to you. The Angels need to deliver a message to you. Open your inner ears and listen for a message of great importance. We exist to *love*. We invite you to reach out and feel the embrace of Heaven. We welcome you into our arms; our soft loving wings await to nurture you and restore your faith.

❖❖❖

Message 43

ANGELS IN NATURE

*H*eaven and Earth are united more than you might realize. Angels live in Heaven, a place and space where the illusion of fear does not exist. Angels live on Earth, a place that is growing closer to Heaven every moment. We are here, incognito, holding the vibration of pure love to help all human minds shift out of the illusion that fear is real. Mother Earth comes from the Twelve Archangel Kingdoms. Father Sun is one of us. The dolphins and orcas of your seas are Cherubim Angels. The giant redwoods are Deva Angels grounding the blueprint for a new Earth. The oceans are an expression of another great Angel. We are your Earth, Water, Air, and Fire. When you need to be reminded of the reality of Angels, visit us in nature.

Nature anchors the Divine Feminine vibration of God. The Divine Feminine is the vessel that holds the Divine Masculine vibration of God. The Divine Masculine directs humanity to take positive action that brings change for the greatest good for humanity and Mother Earth. Nature, in essence, is required for humanity to claim and express divinity. Spending time in nature is the greatest gift that you can give your Soul. Giving thanks for nature is the greatest gift that you can give your ego. Showing that you value Mother Earth by respecting her is a true way to connect with Angels. This connection encourages communication between yourself and all of the Angelic realms.

We thank you for choosing to love Mother Earth and to discover her bounty of Angels. We hold you in a vibration of Divine Oneness. Seek Heaven in nature and open your mind to the higher intelligence all around you.

The following exercise is not to be done in the presence of wild animals because your human vibration might disturb their community. Our exercise takes you into the magical world where your vibration matches that of these great beings.

The Miracle of Nature

Breathe in deeply and exhale deeply. See yourself in an elephant sanctuary. Sit down at the feet of the matriarch elephant. Sing her a love song. Sing to her about your gratitude that she is helping to hold your planet together. Hear and feel the song she sings back to you. Hear and feel the other elephants join in. Ask the elephants to show you their Angelic forms. Embrace the Light they offer. Ask your Divine Feminine and Masculine to fill every cell of your being with the golden Light of love. Share your Light with the elephant Angels.

Message 44

HAPPY CHILDHOOD

*H*uman beings are often deceived into believing that they are all grown up by the time they reach age eighteen, twenty-one, thirty, forty, fifty, sixty, seventy, and beyond. Guardian Angels know better. We are here to tell you that you carry your childhood with you throughout your entire lifetime, whether you realize it or not. Any unfulfilled desires as well as unhealed hurts and resentments stay with you and continue to play out over and over until resolved for your greatest good and highest joy. There is a hurting child that lives within your subconscious as well as a happy child that lives within your heart (superconscious), and these inner child selves are always trying to merge together and become one. We encourage you to get to know both the wounded child and God's Child and together take the journey of creating a new and happy childhood today. The little child within you is your greatest teacher. He or she knows the lessons you still need to master. The child within knows how to bring you what your heart desires and what your body needs.

This fountain of eternal youth within you is the key to transforming the loss of the past and to providing prosperity for the future. The child within you is helping to repair the past by continuing to bring the past to you in different faces and situations. The outcome does not change until you reclaim your self-respect and exchange your powerlessness for strength and wisdom. Let's say that your mother could not love you in the way that you needed to be loved. You can be sure the child within you will bring you relationships that remind you of your relationship with your mother, bringing the same feelings of rejection, loss, and disappointment. The wounded child and the Divine Child work as a team to bring into your life the situations and experiences that feel like a repeat of the past until you forgive, transform, and *love yourself unconditionally.*

In this moment, you have the power to accomplish the inner house-cleaning of all the feelings and memories of being cheated out of what should have been yours. You can forgive the resentment of how life could have been if only you had better parents, or a better education, or a different childhood than the one you were handed. In truth, it was the childhood that you designed and co-created *before you were born.* Changing the past with your creative imagination changes the present and brings new opportunities and blessings into your future.

Come, we will show you how to change the childhood of your past so that you can experience a most happy childhood today!

Creating a Happy Childhood Today

Breathe in deeply and exhale slowly. Close your eyes and take a few unhappy memories from childhood and put them in the color purple. See the violet Fire cleanse the memories until you no longer see them or feel them in your imagination or in your body. Create a new scenario that the child within you desires to experience. Say, "I *allow* myself and the child within me to have a new and happy child-hood *now.*" We invite you to ask again for old memories or feelings of loss and anguish to surface. Once again, wash the scenes of the past with violet Fire and change them into what you desire. Breathe deeply and imagine how you would like your future to look, based on a new foundation of love and happiness.

❖❖❖

Message 45

MAGIC WAND AND CUP

*U*nless you choose otherwise, two archaic ways of thinking can take over your mind and fill your body with anxiety. First is the "old male" paradigm where your ego believes you must be in control of all that is happening, and be able to control future events by requiring the future to work like the past. The second is the "old female" paradigm that supports your ego in being a victim to all of life's disappointments. The "old female" puts your ego in a box that you cannot "think outside of," and your thoughts spin like a hamster playing in a wheel. The "old male" stops the creative flow with his control and sure enough has your ego believing that you are not good enough and rejection is imminent.

We present you with a cure for these outdated and moldy ways of thinking about life: the **wand** and the **cup**. The wand is a symbol for the Divine Masculine's creative power. The cup is a symbol for the Divine Feminine's receptivity to all that is good and brings joy. The Divine Masculine shifts the thinking from control to the truth that God manifests all a human needs through the higher self. The Divine Feminine raises the vibration of the ego being trapped in guilt, blame, and resentment to *feeling and believing* that one can receive God's abundance now. Your Divine Feminine and Divine Masculine support you through the Law of Attraction, the powerful energy of your Soul.

The Law of Attraction brings to you what you hold in your intention. When the old male and old female are sitting in their thrones you attract stress, worry, and the past. When the wand and cup are fixed in your mind's eye you attract what you need to feel safe and happy in the moment. If this is money, then money comes. If this is new work, new work comes. If this is love, love comes. The Divine Masculine and Divine Feminine are the male and female aspects of your Soul and unite your heart and mind with your OverSoul or the bigger part of you that always lives in Heaven. We encourage you to make the choice in any given moment to push out the crusty and moldy and welcome in the fresh and new. Make the choice of the wand and cup!

 ### *Clearing the Throne*

Breathe in. Close your eyes and breathe out any fear, anxiety, or contraction that you feel in your body. Breathe in love, gentleness, and expansion. See a fierce and mean old man sitting on a throne. Next to him sits a pinched and cantankerous old female, also sitting on a throne. They sit together in a small room that has only a tiny window and tiny door. Open the door, lob a violet Fire love bomb into the room, and say, "Enough of your controlling me and making my life miserable!" Watch the violet Fire of transformation and forgiveness fill the room and transform it into a beautiful field that is vast and emerald green. Stuck firmly in the ground is a long staff—Divine Masculine's wand—and next to it, a beautiful cup made of gold with silver trim. Take up your wand and cup and feel the power and love in each. Take a long, deep breath in and out. Say, "I call to me all I need and desire that is for my greatest good and joy *now*." Tap the wand to the ground and visualize what you desire coming into your life. Drink from the cup and feel the satisfaction of receiving all you have asked for and more.

Message 46

CREATIVE LEADERSHIP

*C*reative leadership begins by having the ability to move the hindrances of ego (such as fear, doubt, and control) out of the way so that the mind and heart can focus on the goals that need to be accomplished. These goals are not just about tasks that need to be accomplished or quotas that need to be met. These goals also include helping yourself and others to become better communicators and decision makers.

Whether you work for yourself, work in a team, or work at the top or bottom of an organization, creative leadership can bring you greater success in the areas of your life where it is most needed. When the intuition of the heart is valued above the whining of ego, you can accomplish the "impossible." Today's world demands that you understand success from a deeper and broader perspective. The Twelve Archangels of the Central Soul are the universal supervisors of all leaders and all whom they lead on Earth. We tell you, leader or follower, that success comes best through consciously choosing to surrender the free will of the ego to the higher will of the Soul. Fearful egos that seek power, wealth, and instant gratification are discovering that they end up reaping what they sow: destruction and self-sabotage. Egos that balance logic with intuition evolve into positions of positive influence that come with respect, long-reaching success, and willing cooperation.

Change has come that is happening for the greatest good and professional evolution of all concerned. To support the transformation of your ego self, look inside the library of beliefs that exists within your own mind, and pay attention to how these beliefs become reality in the movie of your work life. When you do not like what you are experiencing, go to the library and throw away the book of lies that has you wrapped up in self-doubt or is creating the experience at work where you are not seen, heard, or valued. We call you to be a leader who uses your creative mind to improve the environment around you by making positive and lasting changes within yourself.

We remind you of choice. It is wise to make decisions based on trusting what your Soul (gut intuition) tells you. Even when the outcome is not what your ego expects, continue to trust that all events happen within divine order. Many situations are not what they appear to be and may need to go through a death before there can be a rebirth and ultimate success. The most respected leaders on Earth know this truth and live it.

We say creative leadership leads to lasting success. Leading with fear begets more fear. Leading with love attracts loyalty, integrity, fame and fortune. Trust us, we know the rules and the time for change in leadership is here and now. Make the choice for positive and productive change and lead on!

 ### Clearing the Shelves

See yourself walk into a big library. The Twelve Archangels are standing amidst all of the big books stacked high on the shelves around you. Ask us to show you which books are lies in disguise. All the books containing beliefs that need to go will glow in neon colors. Say, "I allow all the lies that I have believed in this life or in any other to be transmuted and abolished from my library *now*." Stand back, breathe out the fear and breathe in love and watch the harmful beliefs turn to white dust. All beliefs that serve your greater good and evolution will remain on the shelves.

It is recommended that you come and clear your library when work has become stagnant or when you are feeling taken for granted, overwhelmed, or invisible. Clearing out old beliefs that no longer serve you allows for your Soul and heart to guide you into new and richer success.

Message 47

COMPASSION,
THE HIGHEST VIBRATION

*T*he Great School of Duality, otherwise known as Earth, has a core lesson that all human beings must study and repeat until fully incorporated into their beings. This lesson is the most difficult and often most painful of one's education. You are not allowed to make choices for other adult human beings or to take responsibility for the choices that they make for themselves. Every ego must learn to choose love over fear if they desire to create a joyful, healthy, and balanced life here on Earth.

True compassion is accepting that the best way that you can help another human being is by staying aware of your own vibration. The highest vibration is unconditional love and the lowest is fear. Love and fear both magnify. Love expands, raises, and purifies the lower vibrations within you and all around you. Fear contracts, lowers, and muddies the vibration, but not as much as love can raise it. Angels support you in helping your loved ones by living a compassionate life. A compassionate life asks that you understand how the vibration of your own choices, thoughts, and feelings impact those around you.

For example, when friends or family members are in crisis, show compassion by loving them without going into fear with them. If you climb into the drama with them, then your vibration and energy now supports them in staying in that drama. It will not work for you to rescue your loved one from his drama because we promise that he will only repeat it again. It will not help for you to empathically take her suffering into your own vessel and shower her with sympathy. This will only serve to pull you down into the same abyss. Instead, call on your Guardian Angel to reach into the mind and life of the ones you love and help them to shift their vibration out of fear and contraction into love and expansion. Angels help all those in crisis and chaos through using our vibration. Our vibration of unconditional love raises the vibration of panic and self-pity of the humans we assist so they can make wiser choices. The choice they need to make is presented to them over and over until they get it.

Help us to end suffering on planet Earth by choosing to take responsibility for your own vibration, by being willing to transform any low vibrations, and by respecting your fellow human beings and treating them with real compassion. We are truly grateful for your service to humanity!

 ### *Raising Your Vibration*

Begin by taking in deep breaths of violet Light. Exhale your fears into the violet Light and trust they are transformed into love. Imagine that your fearful, critical, and negative thoughts flow out the top of your head like lava from a volcano. See the lava flow down into a violet Fire ocean and say, "I release, I let go, I choose love." Next, focus on your feelings and allow all of the hurt, anger, denial, shame, and guilt to form a little monster in your belly. His name is "Mr. Grudge." Mr. Grudge can grow as big as he needs to; when he has finished growing, imagine that you push him out of your belly to the left and into the ocean of violet Fire. Say, "Goodbye Mr. Grudge. I choose love and I choose to allow Divine Love to fill me up and heal me *now.*" Now, step into a full bath of water. The water is emerald green, turquoise, and ruby pink. Wash away any left over low vibrations and enjoy feeling the love. Say, "I choose to live a compassionate life today and always!"

Message 48

CHANGING WORLD

*S*ince the beginning, we have walked with you on your journey. As we guide and support you in surrendering to your true self, we ask you to be here now. To evolve into a better life, you must let go of your past; when you hold on to the regrets of the past, you carry them into your future. We desire for you to live a life without regret and without suffering. Today, the Twelve Archangels of the Central Soul give you the message that your world is changing and a most magnificent magic is happening. Humanity is waking up to accepting that change must happen from the inside out. It no longer gives the ego lasting satisfaction to blame others for one's own choices and experiences. Loving yourself and others unconditionally creates the best results— results that last and bring transformation where transformation has never been before. We walk with you out of your past into a new now.

Now is the moment to accept responsibility for your own life and to reach out and help fellow men and women. We say to reach out and help them to help themselves. Love yourself and care for your entire vessel. Make the choice every day to create peace and balance between your ego's will and your heart's truth. As you make this choice, because you are one with every other human being, you help circumvent war in the future. Give thanks for the rich and abundant gifts God has blessed *you* with on this journey. Because you are one with every other human being, doing this helps bring an end to poverty and greed on Earth. Feel your feelings and let go of the hurts and resentments of the past. Because you are one with every other human being, doing this helps doctors and healers to create cures for cancers and other debilitating diseases. Take responsibility for your choices, your thoughts, feelings, and vibration and transform what is low and negative. Because you are one with every other human being, doing this helps to change the effects of global pollution and bring balance back to Mother Earth.

Open your life to transformation and watch the world change for the better. We are happy to share the good news—humanity as a collective is waking up to truth and choosing to believe in love.

Believe that *you* can make a significant difference by changing your belief paradigms. Embrace transformation and allow God to be in charge. It takes only intention, focus, and a little self-discipline of the ego to be in the present, here and now. We thank you for waking up, and we thank you for helping your world to be a safer and healthier home for all concerned!

 New World

Close your eyes and breathe in Divine Mother's ruby pink Light of love. See yourself standing outside a beautiful purple door, Heaven's doorway. Knock at the door until your divine self, the Child of God that lives within you, opens the door. Together, walk down a long flight of stairs into a dark basement. Look for your wounded child or self and ask "What do I need to let go of?" Let it go, and let the Light of God's love fill the basement until it disappears in the Light. Fill up your vessel with Divine Love in all of God's rainbow of loving colors: violet, ruby, sapphire blue, emerald green, turquoise, gold, coral, and white. Grow tall and wide until you can hold the world in your hands. Hold the world in your own loving hands and feel one with the world and your heart. Give thanks for the new world emerging from the old world. Ask God to bless the new world with all she needs and all her children need to live in peace and abundance. Give thanks for all the miracles happening now for your new world!

ANGEL LETTERS

Inspiration for
the Angel Letters

The guidance in the Angel Letters is all about calling on a divine intervention when you need it most. The tenderness of the words work to soothe the hurting ego and help us feel that we are not alone. For example, I have used Archangel Gabriel's method for communication my entire life (see "Letter from Gabriel: Communication"). I just did not realize it until I began working with the Angels all those years ago. Angel communication is an amazing way to bypass ego when we need to get an important message across. In my own experience, Gabriel's communication comes in other forms as well: I have not needed an alarm clock since I learned that Gabriel will blow the trumpet at any hour requested! You may discover for yourself other ways the Angels are here to assist you.

Please turn to the Angel Letters when you need to remember that you are never alone.

Letter from Gabriel
COMMUNICATION

Dear Human Beings,

Human beings seek independence of thought, word, and action and, therefore, usually do not enjoy being told what to think, say, feel, or do. The ego has developed strong protection devices so that even the most heartfelt advice offered by another often falls on deaf ears.

I am Archangel Gabriel, Kingdom of Communication, and I am presenting you with a method to communicate your deepest concerns for other human beings without interfering in their evolution and their destiny. We call this using the Angel Airwave, and we promise miraculous results for the greatest benefit for all concerned.

The Angel Airwave sends your message through thought and emotion to the person with whom you need to communicate. The receiver hears the message as if he thought of the idea or revelation on his own. Human beings don't "get it" until they "know it" from their own higher selves. You and the child of your heart can relax, for you know you have "said" what you need to say. The receiver of your message receives the transmission in God's time according to God's will.

Here is how it works.

Call on Gabriel to open the channel between your OverSoul and the OverSoul of the person with whom you wish to communicate.

Think what you wish to tell the person, don't worry about the words or if the message is too harsh or too gentle, just say it. Open your heart and send love, yes, even if you are completely exasperated with whom you are thinking about.

Gabriel will transmute all negative energy connected with

the message using God's violet Fire of transformation and forgiveness. Know that your message will be sent at just the best moment and will be received just at the peak of the receiver's awareness.

Listen to your intuition, for often you will hear a reply, and you will always receive confirmation from Gabriel that your message was both sent and received, according to God's will, for the greatest good of all.

Express yourself! Don't hold back! Communicate in a way that works, a way in which you can be heard!

I Am always with you!

LOVE,
GABRIEL

Letter from the
Twelve Archangel Kingdoms

CHILDREN AND
THEIR GUARDIAN ANGELS

Dear Human Beings,

It is easier for newly born infants to see their Guardian Angels than it is for them to see anything in physical form on Earth. Their Angels play with them and surround them in God's love. Their Guardian Angels help their Souls to make the transition in vibration between Heaven and Earth and adjust to being in a tiny body. Babies sleep so they can grow, and they sleep so their Angels can help them adjust to their new environment, an environment where fear's shabungi is still present.

As infants grow into toddlers, their Guardian Angels are just as present, although now the babies are more distracted by what is happening in the physical world. Babies must learn how to communicate again with spoken words instead of just communicating with thought and Heaven's music.

The toddler and preschooler can still see and feel their Angels with ease and often address them as invisible playmates. These playmates do not break things or say anything hurtful. The child's ego is attempting to create separation and already trying out control and avoiding responsibility. The Guardian Angels are not allowed to interfere in the separation because the Soul has come to experience fear and then transmute it in life.

The more imaginative the child stays, the more real and alive the child's Guardian Angels stay. We are hopeful you will encourage your children to keep their imagination open!

Ask your children about their Angels, and they will tell you all about their friends of Light and Sound. Encourage them to call on their Guardian Angels for assistance and for entertainment when bored or lonely.

🏵️ Imagery Exercise to Do with Your Children

Sit together in a comfortable room. Have soothing, enjoyable music softly playing in the background. Close your eyes, and both of you imagine you are sitting in a giant bubble of pink Light. Breathe, and welcome your Guardian Angels to come and tell you their names.

What colors are they wearing, and what do they look like? Remember they may look different from what you might expect. Ask them anything you like. When you are ready, open your eyes, and share your experiences with each other.

Call on your Guardian Angels for all things great and small. Nothing is too big or too little to ask your Angel to help you with. Angels always follow God's Law of One. This means we will do only what is for the greatest joy and good of all people and all God's Creation.

We are real! We are all around you! Call out to us and know Mother Father God loves you always!

LOVE AND JOY TO YOU,
THE TWELVE ARCHANGELS

P.S. Dear Parents,

Guardian Angels are the most loving counselors. Remind your children to call on their Angels for any tragic event such as the loss of a pet or loved one. Angels can assist in calming and reassuring your child during times of stress for the family and during major transitions. Send your child's Guardian Angels to school each day. Remember, your child's Soul does know what it must experience, and Angels can help these lessons be mastered with gentleness.

Letter from the
Twelve Archangel Kingdoms

MANAGING CRISIS

Dear Human Beings,

For any crisis or stressful situation, we recommend the following:

Breathe in deeply and exhale slowly. Call on your Angels and say, "I surrender." Tell your Angels what you need in the present moment. Be as specific as possible.

Breathe.

Keep your mind on the present. Say, "I Am calling on the will of God."

Breathe and trust all is in divine order. We are with you! We are with you always!

After the crisis is over, sit or lie down and ask your Angels, Divine Male, Divine Female, and God's Child inside your heart, "Why did I create this, and what do I need to discover about myself here in this situation?"

 ### *Understanding Crisis*

Breathe in deeply and exhale slowly. Imagine that you are observing your crisis as if you are watching a movie on the big screen. Master Fear is the character teaching you much about yourself and where you give your power away. Master Fear is actually an Angel in disguise. Fear gives you an opportunity to trust in God, completely. See yourself facing Master Fear. Ask him why he is testing you in this way. Ask him, "What must I learn from my discomfort to change the movie and stop this crisis?" Now, change the movie. Redirect the events in the movie so that you are the hero in the scene. Say, "I Am willing to experience the miracle of this crisis ending. I Am grateful to have it behind me."

Guided Imagery Exercise for Those Who Help Others in Crisis

Breathe in slowly and exhale completely. Repeat until you feel calm and centered. Say, "I Am one with God." Surround yourself with white gold Light of Divine Love and protection. Immediately ask us to send God's love and healing to the person in need. See the other person in white gold Light and ask to know where this person is caught in fear. Say, "I call on Archangel Michael to help this person see his or her truth."

When you are helping those in crisis, maintain a sacred space and remember not to get enticed into the drama. Every experience is created by the OverSoul to help the human Soul evolve. The people you are trying to help need to be willing to help themselves or they will only repeat the crisis.

Tell us exactly how you perceive the situation from your human perspective, and tell us how we can help your client, friend, or loved one. Trust that all is in divine order. We will respond immediately to your request for assistance. Miracles are everywhere you look for them, and miracles happen in abundance.

As you see miracles manifest to help in crisis situations, your faith grows. We recommend that you see the value in asking your OverSoul for experiences that help your faith grow without crisis. You are the creator of your reality. If you can transform fear into love without experiencing crisis, celebrate! Fear is a magnificent tool for building trust and faith in God. Remember, it is only a tool, and often Divine Love can work just as well, if not better, for building trust and faith in God. When you take Divine Love and Oneness for granted, you can be sure fear is around the corner to help you learn more about the infinite power of God.

LOVE AND POSITIVE CHANGE,

THE TWELVE ARCHANGELS

Letter from the *Twelve Archangel Kingdoms*

DEPRESSION AND PAIN

Dear Human Beings,

Human beings can become most uncomfortable when they do not receive what they hope for at the time they want their desire to manifest. Depression usually happens when humans feel hopeless because their life seems to be staying in the same stagnant experience.

We present you with our remedy for alleviating discomfort and dissatisfaction.

 Surrender to Love

Close your eyes and imagine you are resting in the loving arms of your Guardian Angel. Breathe in immortal love in a rainbow of colors. Breathe in hope and demand God's divine rescue. Surrender to your discomfort. Know it is almost over.

Yell and scream and blow up your life in God's violet Fire of transformation. It is almost over, this discomfort. Know you are clearing pain and unhappiness for all people everywhere. Know it is leaving and you are learning and remembering with each painful feeling that *God is real* and you are one with God.

Ask your Angels to help you. See the bright Light at the end of the tunnel of your depression.

Hold our hands for we are always with you. Today is a great day for a miracle!

LOVE AND PEACEFUL SURRENDER,

THE TWELVE ARCHANGELS

The Archangels Glossary

Understanding
the Language of the Angels

I created the glossary with the intention of making Angelic guidance easy to understand and digest. It is my experience that we define words based on our past experiences. It was important to me, and to the Twelve Archangels, that the reader feel completely supported in connecting with the truth of the information. Understanding the language is invaluable for this purpose.

Angel: Being of pure Divine Love whose purpose is to nurture and assist, obeying the Law of One (in a manner that is for the greatest good for all the Universe).

Archangel: Messenger for God's will assigned the task of bringing the human race home to the heart of Mother Father God. Archangels are protectors and guides for all healers called to assist others or called to heal Mother Earth. Teachers of our lessons here on schoolroom Earth.

ascension: Achieving freedom from fear in your mind and merging with your divine self, while in your human body. Living on Earth in Heaven's vibration of unconditional, full-time love.

aura: Radiating energy field surrounding each body (spiritual, mental, emotional, and physical) of the vessel. The aura's colors give information on the health status of each body. The aura colors of the spiritual body give information on the life purpose and God service of the human being.

body of Light and Sound: Spiritual body vibrating at the frequency of pure love (no fear). The body of Light and Sound consists of God's energy from the Central Soul of God. Also called the *OverSoul.*

Butterfly Angels: Angels that help with transformation of fears. This Angelic Kingdom is involved in transportation within the realms of Heaven.

center: The still, quiet, and satisfied place inside the mind, called the "heart." The center is the home of God within the human vessel, and it is the place of feeling content and united with all of God's Creation. In the center, the mind can open and connect with the intuition and personal truth. Same as *heart center.*

Central Soul (Sun): The center point of the heart of Mother Father God, Divine Love, and Creation. This is the sacred space where Mother Father God births each particle of God's energy, making up the Universe.

chakra: Energy center supplying God's Divine Love to the spiritual, mental, emotional, and physical bodies. Chakras work like automobile batteries in that they need to be fully charged and in alignment with the higher self and vessel. Each chakra's energy has a different focus for healing the mental, emotional, and physical bodies.

Cherubim: The Angelic Kingdom of the Divine Mother. All-loving and all-powerful Angels that support healing and positive change through the nurturing of the feminine within all human beings and planet Earth.

chi: The life force energy generated by the Soul through the Nature Angel to create and nourish the physical body.

Child of God, Divine Child, God Child, or God's Child: The all-believing, all-trusting, totally free, and beautiful child inside your heart. God's Child brings in Divine Love from the OverSoul and gives love to the ego self and shadow self, as well as the mental, emotional, and physical bodies.

child within: See *inner child.*

coral orange Flame or Light: The Angel power of Soul, united with the OverSoul. The energy of creativity, kundalini, and chi. Also the fuel for the higher functioning of the Law of Attraction.

Creation: God's energy in Light and Sound vibrating at a frequency where the perceiver sees the energy as tangible with taste, touch, feel, audible sound, sight, or knowing. Mother Earth and all her inhabitants are examples of Creation.

creation energy: Energy that unifies thought, emotion, and love and generates physical matter, such as stars, planets, human beings, animals, plants, and rocks.

crown chakra: The chakra of spiritual energy located at the top of the head. This chakra is home to violet Light or Fire, the Angel power of transformation and forgiveness.

cup: Symbol for the Divine Feminine and a receptacle for holding Divine Love, Divine Mother's love.

Deva: An Angel who designs physical creation and lowers the vibration of God's energy to achieve manifestation of the physical form. Devas design planets and human bodies and all that is physical.

Divine: The truth and love and will of Mother Father God resonating at the highest and purest vibration of Sound and Light, *unconditional love.*

Divine Child: See *Child of God.*

divine destiny: Destiny is the experience of achieving the peace of being connected with Oneness, all that exists in the Universe. When karmic debt is transformed, you can experience the confidence of knowing who you are and what your highest purpose is on Earth.

divine grace: An unexpected gift of insight, forgiveness, or understanding. Grace is Mother Father God's way of showing affection. The ultimate fulfillment of living life from the center.

divine intervention: The act of Mother Father God to intercede on behalf of humanity, through the Law of One, to bring relief from the impact of fear. Also, a divine act of Angels to bring miracles into daily life for the purpose of ending suffering and to resolve crisis. Humanity is invited to ask for a divine intervention when needed.

divine law: God's laws supersede all human law. Divine justice serves from the heart of God and always manifests according to God's will and for the highest joy and greatest good of the Universe.

Divine Love: The vibration of all of God's energy. Divine Love is the expression of Oneness with all Divine Thought, Emotion, and Creation. Divine Love is God, and God is Divine Love. Divine Love is the force that holds the Universe together.

divine order: Mother Father God's plan for the Earth and Universe perfectly orchestrated by God's will in God's time. All events in Earth's history have unfolded according to divine order. It is divine order for Earth and Heaven to be one.

duality: The separation of human thought, emotion, and creation from Oneness with God. Duality creates the illusion of fear in opposition to the reality of truth of Divine Love.

Earth: A manifestation of God's Creation existing at the present moment. Planet Earth is the schoolroom for all Souls needing to experience duality for their evolution. Planet Earth's vibration—because of fearful thoughts—is lower (less clear) than the vibration of Heaven. Earth's vibration is purified constantly and is rapidly returning to the vibration of Divine Love.

ego: The part of the human mind capable of believing that self is separate from God and lives independently from the rest of Oneness (lives outside of the Universe). The ego defines the human personality in relationship to other people and the surrounding world.

emerald green Light or Fire: The Angel power of the heart chakra united with God's heart. See also *heart chakra.*

emotion: Mother God's Holy Spirit giving the power to manifest Divine Thought into the creation of experiences on Earth.

emotional body: The body where the human being stores unacknowledged and unprocessed feelings. When the emotional body is clear, it is the heart center and the place of Oneness within the human self.

energy: Light and Sound, Mother Father God's energy of Divine Love. Energy creates all God's Universe, formed and unformed. The word "energy" is sometimes used to mean a function or direction of God's Divine Love. Healing energy is an example of God's energy having a specific purpose and direction. Negative energy would mean the Light and Sound are contaminated with fear; see *shabungi.*

evolution: The continuous learning and breaking out of fearful thought. Evolution is the process of returning the human vessel—through raising the vibration of thought, memory, beliefs, and feelings—back to the vibration and consciousness of Heaven.

faith: The opposite of control is trust. Having faith in God begins with a sincere intention to trust in Mother Father God's divine plan and an ever-deepening knowing that love is all there is.

Father God: The masculine aspect of God, which generates Light and Divine Thought energy. May be referred to as *Divine Masculine.*

fear: Deceptive and low vibration human thought-energy, creating the illusion that humans are separate from God.

feeling: Messages from the mental body or from the spiritual body to the mental body describing where Holy Spirit (or emotion) is blocked, or flowing, in the human vessel. Feelings are also messages telling the human mind what he or she desires to experience.

Flame: Chakra energy united with Angel power to facilitate transformation, awakening, and healing. Flame means the same as *energy.* See also *God.*

fuchsia with indigo Flame: The healing energy of the third eye chakra that looks like a sunrise. The fuchsia with indigo Flame opens the intuition channels for seeing, hearing, knowing, and sensing beyond the physcial plane.

God: All there is and all there ever shall be. God is energy, and this energy is both Light and Sound. God's Light and Sound generate Divine Love, and Divine Love creates God's Creation and the Universe. God is the same as *Source* and *Creator.*

God Child: See *Child of God.*

greatest good: Benefits all particles of God's energy (the entire Universe) as well as all human beings, nature, and the evolution of all human Souls.

Great School of Duality: The school of opposites created by the Twelve Archangels to teach human beings the value of choosing love.

Guardian Angels: Angels that protect human beings in each incarnation and travel with you throughout your life. Their job is to support without interference, unless a divine intervention is requested and approved by the OverSoul. They guard your Soul's umbilical cord connecting your Soul to your OverSoul while you are attending the Great School of Duality.

Guide: A loving being working together with the OverSoul to offer reassurance and direction to the Soul traveling on Earth. Guides are your teachers and loved ones now living in Heaven.

healing: The clearing of fear from any part of the human vessel.

heart chakra: Heaven's doorway within the human being and home to the Divine Child. The Angel power of unconditional love and healing, especially useful for helping the wounded child to let go of the past.

Heaven: A reality where fear does not exist. Heaven is the vibration of Oneness and pure Divine Love, the sacred space that Earth is evolving into.

higher self: See also *OverSoul*. The bigger part of the human being that lives in Heaven and directs the lessons for the ego and Soul while attending the Great School of Duality.

highest joy: The most all-encompassing and euphoric joy expressed by the heart center. Highest joy is experienced when human beings are united with Mother Father God's Divine Love. Highest joy is felt by all particles of God's energy throughout the Universe.

Holy Spirit: Mother God's Sound in the form of Divine Emotion. Red Fire of God's Divine Love in all shades of red and pink, bringing unconditional love, compassion, and freedom.

home: The heart center when the human ego mind is quiet and the human vessel feels completely united with mind, heart, body, and Soul. Home also means experiencing the vibration of Heaven and Oneness with all of God's Creation.

human being: A Child of God seeking to return to Oneness. A student attending the Great School of Duality and needing to learn how to bring more Heaven into everyday life.

I Am: The center of the heart of God where all of God's Creation is one, the Central Soul, and the origin of all that is formed and unformed. "I Am" defines the human center and is the alpha and omega of God's energy. See also *Universe*.

imagination: The doorway to experiencing spiritual clairvoyance and receiving and sending visual messages to God and to God's Creation. Imagination may also be called "seeing." Imagination is vital to receiving creative genius ideas from the OverSoul and Guides. Activation of the clear, divine, and intuitive imagination is dependent on connecting with God's Child within your heart.

inner child: God's Child wrapped in all the human experiences creating the illusion of abandonment by Mother Father God during this lifetime on Earth. Connecting with the inner child offers access to buried memories and belief systems stored in the deep subconscious.

intuition: Knowing, sensing, visual, or auditory messages coming from the spiritual body, Soul, or OverSoul, usually relayed as images or words to the mental body, feelings to the emotional body, and sensations to the physical body. A "gut reaction" is the intuition at work.

karma: Incomplete lessons from schoolroom Earth that must be learned and balanced for the ego, through the Soul, to continue evolving into a state of Oneness with all Creation.

kundalini energy: The combined and integrated energies of the Fire of the Soul together with the chi or life force. As the human evolves, the force of the kundalini connects directly with the Light and Sound of the OverSoul.

Law of One: The law stating that all God's Children are influenced by the thoughts, feelings, and actions of all people. If any particles of God's energy are harmed or vibrating at a frequency less than Divine Love, all of God experiences this disharmony. Likewise, when any particles of God's energy experience healing and balancing, the Universe benefits. The Law of One governs the positive results that happen when any human helps himself or herself to evolve and trust in God's love.

life force: The chi energy produced by the Nature Angel holding the human vessel in physical form and giving life to all the cells of the physical body.

Light: Divine Thought, Mother Father God's Divine Love directed for the purpose of healing human consciousness, both individual and global. In this text, Light is synomous with *Divine Love.*

Lucifer Michael, Archangel: Kingdom of God's united Light and willpower. The Archangel Lucifer Michael split into two Angelic Kingdoms in order to create the illusion of separation and fear on planet Earth.

manifestation: The final step in the process of creation on Earth. Bringing a creative idea to fruition, the actual fulfillment of experiencing a miracle. Manifestation of money would be the moment the actual physical money is in sight.

master: A being totally connected with the spiritual self and living free of fear in the mental, emotional, and physical bodies.

mental body: The body of the vessel creating and receiving thought.

Michael's Fire or Flame: The energy produced by the will (throat) chakra fused with God's energy of truth and awareness. Michael's Flame burns through deception and karmic debt. It also is important for healing the physical body and for providing strength and courage when needed to face life's challenges.

miracle: A magical moment of awareness of receiving and/or experiencing exactly what is needed for the greatest good of all concerned. A miracle can also be a gift of clear insight.

Mother God: The female aspect of God generating Sound and Divine Emotion. Mother God's energy is Holy Spirit, the Fire of unconditional love and compassion for all God's Creation. Mother Earth is a representation (Angel) of Mother God.

music: The most potent healing energy of the Universe. Angels can best be defined as divine music. God's divine music is both Sound and Light delivered at the vibration of Oneness. Angels multiply when greater help is needed, just like turning up the volume when music is being played.

Nature Angel: The Angel of Creation that holds the chi, life force, together at the Earth's vibration that gives the human being a physical form. At death, the Nature Angel takes the Soul back to Heaven and creates a new vessel at the vibration of Heaven.

Oneness: To be completely united with all particles of God's energy and all of God's Creation.

OverSoul: The spiritual body of the human vessel still remaining inside of Oneness and the vibration of Heaven. The OverSoul is the higher self, communicating through the intuitive mind, that directs the Soul on the evolutionary path home to God.

physical body: Temple of Divine Love holding the precious human being's thought and emotion. The physical body is the container existing at the densest vibration of God's energy on Earth, and the body requiring the highest quality and quantity of God's energy for complete healing.

respect: A vibration of Divine Love that facilitates the raising up of the human self to the divine self. The gift from divine grace that helps the wounded ego surrender to the direction of the Soul and OverSoul.

root chakra: The center of spiritual energy located at the bottom of the spine that is home to Divine Mother's love, or the Holy Spirit. This is the tribal or ancestral chakra that when used correctly brings healing to ancestors and future generations. The root chakra stores the survival belief paradigms.

ruby Flame or Fire: The same energy as the Holy Spirit only softened in intensity. The Angel power that supports receiving abundance from Source.

sapphire blue Flame or Fire: The Angel power of truth and awareness. The same as Michael's Flame. See also *will chakra.*

see: Using the creative mind, which houses the imagination, to create healing images in one's mind. To "see" in this text is the same as to visualize or to imagine.

separation: The illusion that human beings live outsde of God's Central Soul. Separation causes the experience on Earth that fear is real and has power over the divine destiny of the human being.

shabungi: Negative or low vibration energy that is made from thought and powered with emotion. Shabungi is the same as darkness or evil.

shadow: The shadow is the deceptive, self-sabotaging, and fearful aspect of the ego that often remains hidden until the mental self opens and begins the process of healing. Violet Fire transforms the shadow self into the God self. The shadow can offer great insight into hidden lies and misconceptions that you believe but that do not serve you.

solar plexus chakra: The center of spiritual energy responsible for personal power and confidence. The Angel power of magnetic love that supports creating better self-esteem and happiness.

Soul: Emissary of the OverSoul incarnating on Earth to heal karma and transform fear back into love. The source within the human being of creativity and ideas of creative genius quality.

Soul chakra (or sexual chakra): The center of spiritual energy generating the sacred kundalini and chi. The Angel power of creativity. The source of the coral orange Flame within the human being.

Sound: Divine Emotion generating an all-powerful, all-loving clearing and healing force required for human evolution and freedom. God's Sound and Light are always fused and create Holy Spirit, the Fire of Mother God's unconditional love.

spiritual body: Body of Sound and Light uniting the OverSoul with the Soul. The spiritual body houses the chakras and provides all healing energies needed to achieve complete freedom of the human vessel on Earth.

subconscious and deep subconscious: Memories and beliefs that orginate from the past that are pushed down into hiding. This storage place is also referred to as "the cellar" or "the basement" by the Twelve Archangels.

superconscious: The part of the mind that connects with the spiritual realms, especially the Divine Child within. The intelligence of the intuition.

third eye chakra: Energy center located in the center of the brain, which is responsible for receiving and sending all intuitive communication. The Angel power of the fuchsia and indigo Flame for seeing, hearing, knowing, and sensing beyond the confines of illusion.

thought: The male aspect of God's energy allowing for the conception of all Creation. Thought is the universal communicator between all particles of God's energy.

transformation: Alchemical process of raising the vibration of thought to the highest level of unconditional love. The experience of changing fear into love and death (change) into life (new beginning). Divine transformation can be used to achieve greater awareness and freedom from fear and fear's illusions.

trust: An ongoing process of using positive intention to support the ego in first believing and then experiencing unconditional and constant support from Mother Father God.

truth: The alignment of physical, emotional, mental, and spiritual knowing of the human mind with the higher self (superconscious).

turquoise Flame or Light: The Angel power coming from the fusion of the will and heart chakras, which facilitates the manifestation of success and dreams coming true. A Flame that reminds you of the power of gratitude and joy.

Twelve Archangels of the Central Soul (Sun): All-loving and all-powerful musical conductors/ Angels of Mother Father God's energy holding the vision and destiny of humanity's freedom from Master Fear. Founders and participating faculty of the Great School of Duality.

Universe: All that God has created; Oneness, Creation, Source.

vessel: The energy field or protecting aura holding God's energy of Creation in a physical body that appears to be solid and finite. The human being.

victim-consciousness: Conscious, subconscious, or deep subconscious belief in abandonment by Mother Father God, another human being, or Mother Earth. The refusal to take responsibility for creating one's own reality on Earth and the belief that this reality is unchangeable.

violet Fire: Light and Sound generated by the crown chakra, catalyzing transformation of fearful thought into loving thought. The all-loving power of forgiveness that frees the ego from his or her past.

visualization: The action of creating a mental image of the self, another person, or an experience for the purpose of healing the vessel. Same as to *see* and *imagination*.

wand (or magic wand): The wand is a metaphor for Divine Masculine confidence, strength, manifesting power, and positive, all-loving force.

will: Mother Father God's divine plan to bring all humanity back to a state of Oneness with God. Will is the manifestation of inner strength to trust in God and transform fear back into love. The will of ego is what drives the human being to want instant gratification, even if what is desired will bring harm or disappointment. The Twelve Archangels recommend surrendering the free will of ego to the higher will of the OverSoul.

will chakra (or throat chakra): The center of spiritual energy responsible for communicating the truth at the highest vibration. The Angel power of Archangel Michael's truth, courage, awareness, and justice.

white Fire or Light: The Angel power of purification and protection. This energy comes from the OverSoul and the Central Sun. When mixed with gold Light, it becomes the white gold Light of Divine Love.

white gold Light: The Light and Sound of Divine Love. White gold Light may be referred to as the Christ-Buddha energy.

wounded child: The child self within you that holds the memory of hurt and loss from childhood. The wounded child is the same as the subconscious aspect of ego.

Index